THE SHAMAN'S WIFE

T0281986

THE SHAMAN'S WIFE

Alicia M. Rodriguez

SHE WRITES PRESS

Published 2024
Printed in the United States of America
Print ISBN: 978-1-64742-756-6
E-ISBN: 978-1-64742-757-3
Library of Congress Control Number: 2024907100

For information, address:
She Writes Press
1569 Solano Ave #546
Berkeley, CA 94707

Interior Design by Kiran Spees

She Writes Press is a division of SparkPoint Studio, LLC.

Names and identifying characteristics have been changed to protect the privacy of certain individuals.

CONTENTS

INTRODUCTION

Somewhere it's written that you will do things, meet people, and go places you never thought you would, and dive headfirst into the murky waters of the unknown. In some liminal space, choices are not made, roads are not taken, and a reality you once dreamed was yours now only exists as a regret for what might've been. Life has you choose between door number one, door number two, and door number three, barking out the numbers like a talk show host. The crowd screams, "Pick one! Pick two! Pick three!" Finally, you muster the courage and pick your door while believing you control that choice. The door swings open, and no, it's not a cruise; it's a kayak on the Chesapeake Bay.

You learn to love your choices.

At nineteen, I lose my innocence about the world when my father, who keeps me safe, dies suddenly. My family is now broken and impoverished. I decide not to return to college, only to find out that an anonymous donor has paid for my tuition and will continue to pay it for the three years until I graduate. Years later, a boozy wedding reveals the mystery donor, someone I had never met but who thought enough of me to ensure my education because his niece, my friend, told him I deserved more.

On the darkest night in the middle of a violent storm, I approach a rocky precipice, ready to take that one last step into oblivion, driven by the inevitable relief that comes from a deathly silence, from heartbreak, and the unrelenting pain in my body and soul. But as the wild wind threatens to rip away my clothes and my life, I hear the pleading voice of my child begging me to stay. So I return, empty, surrendering to a life I didn't know I wanted, soaked through and through by salt, rain, and tears.

A mere two words, rising unbidden from my throat, mean the end to a twenty-one-year marriage that I thought would last forever. Hope vanishes like a puff of smoke, leaving behind the odor of hurt, grief, and bitterness.

The dog I adopt is my only true guru, saving me from the nights I'm on my knees, barfing my tequila-fueled sorrow into the porcelain god in the bathroom.

A simple decision made on a whim becomes a life-changing encounter with an unseen world that takes me into a life that feels both alien and familiar. Love arrives like a shooting star across the heavens—brilliant, unexpected, pointing me toward the uncharted territory of the universe. I'm drawn by destiny to a land steeped in mystery and spirituality, where the ancestors are guides and sacred truths spring from the crystalline rivers, the snowcapped mountains, and the vast expanse of the ocean. An ancient ceremony amid ancestral ruins on top of a grass-covered pyramid offers the promise of eternal love from the Andean shaman who later becomes my husband.

Without money or a plan, I find a sacred space on a fallow hillside, a seed planted in the dirt that dares life to emerge. The ongoing conversation between the mountain and ocean speaks to a secret portal to other dimensions. This battleground of spiritual warfare coexists with sacred rituals that dare me to cross to the other side and meet myself, shadow and light enmeshed, while I cautiously learn to dance between the spiritual and secular worlds.

In many ways, my life feels like a pilgrimage, its events leading me step-by-step to where I am today, a place I never expected to be. I can now see how each incident transformed who I am and continues to transform who I am becoming. Each person has chiseled away at any mask I may have created to protect myself from sorrow and pain. The longing I have felt all my life has driven me to explore through books, travel, and deeper conversations with people I never imagined I would know. Priests, shamans, artists, healers, writers, poets, adventurers, and rebels have all left their mark on me. I have discovered the power of cocreating beauty and magic with others.

I call these collaborations *encuentros*, or encounters. Encounters occur when the full power and creative force of two or more beings are at play. Since there are no scripts or instructions, there are also no assurances. These encounters hold the life-giving energy of stars when they meet with their full force, exploding into a new nebula of light and energy. My *encuentro* changed the course of my life and, like two colliding stars, destroyed and then transformed me.

In April 2012, I arrived in Ecuador to attend a meeting I was unprepared for but destined to experience. I intuitively recognized my guide in an unassuming man with long black hair tucked into a baseball cap. I would learn about shamanism, mysticism, and the unseen spiritual world for the next eight years. Most importantly, I would learn about myself and recover my soul's mystery in Ecuador's Andean wisdom traditions.

This encounter marked the portal to an inner world I had explored as a child and had left behind as an adult. I was coming home, but I didn't yet know it. It would take eight years of stepping one foot in front of the other, sometimes knowing what was ahead—more often, not—and trusting that each day would reveal my life to me in new ways.

The illusion that we know where our lives are going is a belief we carry unconsciously. We're not prepared for the whimsical decision that seems insignificant at the moment but changes our life forever.

In his poem "The Road Not Taken," Robert Frost writes, "Two roads diverged in a wood, and I— / I took the one less traveled by / And that has made all the difference." Those lines echo across time, repeating like the voice that carries over a canyon. I took the road less traveled, and it most certainly made all the difference.

– 1 –
DANCING BETWEEN THE WORLDS

Between the slats of the wooden window shutters, long fingers of moonlight seep into the bedroom, casting a soft glow. No abrupt ringing of a clock nor the cock-a-doodle-doo of the neighbor's rooster—the one I often threaten to strangle—can awaken me like this gentle luminescence.

Lying beside me on the bed, my husband is a bulky mass under the covers, his curly black hair tumbling onto his pillow. His breathing is interrupted by an occasional snore rising from his throat and the *clink-clink* sound of the ceiling fan, its small metal chain hitting metal on repeat. Our shared cotton sheet rises and falls with the billowing of the mosquito netting covering our bed. The room pulses with a rhythm, like a lung: in, out, in, out.

The door, slightly ajar, allows the air to escape, swirling through the narrow spaces around the wooden chest of drawers, two night-stands, and double bed that are wedged into our bedroom. I hear rus-tling between the bamboo ceiling and the ceramic roof, loud enough to startle me. I try hard not to imagine what it might be. The illumi-nated dial of the clock perched on the dresser reads 3:45 a.m. Not even the crickets are awake.

The mosquito net amplifies the heat and humidity, leaving me struggling to breathe. Pulling myself up on the damp pillows, I watch him. My mind is flooded with memories of our first months together, when I would travel to Ecuador to be with him. I can still recall the comfort of the wool blankets covering us on Andes nights so cold that I could sometimes see our breath merge as we fell asleep. Such a difference from the heaviness I now feel in this bedroom on the coast. Such a distance between then and now, he and I.

Those early months were full of anticipation of what our lives could become. We were two people from opposite worlds trying to find one another. He was born in nature, educated by ancestral stories teaching that sacred waterfalls are the source of wisdom, healing comes from the medicinal plants of the rainforest, and enlightenment is found through conversations with the spirit world. Bolivar, whom everyone calls Napo, is a sixth-generation shaman. His father had secretly advised presidents, and for years his mother had sold candy and wisdom from a cart in a gang-ridden neighborhood in Quito. His brother Carlos had followed a shamanic vision to visit the Lakota in South Dakota and eventually settled in Annapolis, Maryland, where he lived with his wife, Megan, a friend of mine. She introduced me to Carlos, the beginning of a string of events that led me to this land on the coast.

I met Carlos at a time when my life balanced precariously between success and failure. Over the years, I'd built a thriving business in personal development and leadership. Running from client to client in my Michael Kors suits and Dior slingbacks, I found my life was held together by lattes and a mobile phone. My natural rhythm had adapted to the twelve-hour days typical of an entrepreneur. I was well-suited to my work, always curious about how humans think, feel, and act. I enjoyed listening to the thousands of stories my clients would tell me, helping them finally become the authors of their lives. Seeing people shift into alignment with their hearts inspired me. It also increased an insistent nagging, an uneasiness that I could not define, suggesting a drifting in my own life.

My intense business life was offset by the beauty of living on the

Chesapeake Bay surrounded by neighbors I considered close friends. On the bay, kayaking became my meditation and my escape into my elusive inner world, a stillness on the water that I could integrate into my body and soul. Those moments paddling through the waves were precious to me, a way to stay connected to my senses and the natural world that sustained me during a difficult time.

As I succeeded in my career, my personal life fell apart. My husband and I had grown apart after a friendship of fifteen years and then a twenty-one-year marriage. Battered by economic failures, job losses, and both our mothers being ravaged by dementia, we had lost our homes and our faith in each other. In 2010, we separated. My most significant loss was my son, who remained with his father—a man of integrity and the role model our son needed as he grew into young adulthood. While cooking dinner for one on dark winter nights as the wind howled over the bay, I questioned if I had done the right thing. *Could I have done more? Should I go back to my marriage? Will my son blame me for the rest of his life?* These questions haunted me, and no amount of wine would erase them.

Tonight, my sleep is disturbed by that same nagging feeling I remember from years ago. I lift the mosquito net just enough to sit on the edge of the bed, dangling my feet. Like most artisanal bungalows in Ecuador, the construction quality is rough, resulting in uneven floors and warped walls that leave gaps to the outside. Once, when the house was still newly built, I heard scuffling under the bed. An unidentified furry rodent emerged, dragging a tarantula into the corner of the room. After that, I poured concrete into every hole I could find. Who knew that mice could eat through it? Like Sisyphus and his boulder, my efforts to keep these openings plugged were futile. Now, I find my slippers and hold them between two fingers, shaking them before slipping them onto my feet. I have learned never to put my feet into shoes without checking for intruders.

Tiptoeing to the bathroom door, I pull my black silk robe off the hanger. It sticks to my skin until the air from the ceiling fan lifts it away from my body. Then I move slowly to the door, avoiding the boards that creak the most. I gingerly pull it closed so as not to wake him.

From the bedroom, I enter the open space of the kitchen, living room, and dining room. A large glass balcony door replaces the west wall, revealing a stunning view of the Pacific Ocean glowing under the full moon. Shadows dance between the swaying palm trees and adobe dwellings in the valley below. "There must be a breeze," I whisper. Looking south toward town, I see a few deserted buildings with open windows that look like gaping mouths silenced by the night.

My body aches as if I have strained every muscle, reminding me of the effort it took to build here on this remote swath of land. I run my hand over the counter, which feels surprisingly cool, remembering how I'd asked my husband to use only one sheet of granite. Instead, he used sheets of composite granite to save money, grouting them together unevenly. An L-shaped jigsaw of fake stone held together with ribbons of stained grout replaces the countertop I had planned.

Under it, a deep concrete shelf holds pots, pans, and plates, some so far back that I can't see them in the darkness. A six-burner gas stove-top sits on the shorter end of the counter. A long rubber tube connects it to a rusting gas tank partially hidden in the nook underneath.

With a muffled thud, I fall into the low sofa in the middle of the room, facing the ocean. On sleepless nights, I sit here quietly watching the stars as if their sparkle might comfort me, but tonight the sky is obscured by the magnificence of the bright moon.

A glint in the kitchen catches my eye. I keep a bottle of Aguardiente Antioqueño on a shelf, a clear alcohol made in Colombia and named firewater for a good reason. I grew up in a Colombian family, and we always had aguardiente in the house. My mother would say it was for medicinal reasons. With its silver label, red lettering, and blue cap, the bottle is well recognized in South America.

This is my prescription for restless nights. I pour myself more than

I should, anticipating its numbing effects. "This will help me sleep," I rationalize as I grab my glass and tuck the bottle under my arm. The floorboards creak as I tiptoe toward the front door, closing it lightly behind me. Taking a deep breath outside reminds me of coming up for air under the ocean's surface. My body begins to unwind. Chief and Bella, my rescue dogs, peer at me from their beds on the porch. They were only about four months old when I saw a posting on a rescue site looking for anyone who might want to adopt them. Chief is a medium-sized tan-and-brown dog with a strong hunting instinct. He can run faster than any dog I have ever seen. Bella is a short, stocky black dog with a long, muscular body, ears like a bat, and soulful eyes that melt hearts. They have been with us for two years, the guardians and the clowns of the quinta.

At night, they sleep in plastic tubs on our house's small porch. With their tails wagging, they join me as I walk to the brick path that leads to the driveway. Imposing palm and coconut trees line the four-hundred-meter-long driveway that divides the top and middle levels. Tall irises and blooming bushes add vermilion, persimmon, and goldenrod splashes to the entryway beyond the handmade guayacan portico that serves as the gate to the property. The blossoms are vibrant in the moonlight, colorful companions pointing toward the upper terrace, where I arrive at the alfresco kitchen table with my glass and bottle. I pause to refill my drink and then take the warm liquid into my mouth, savoring the anisette sweetness.

Like ghosts, memories of past guests fill the kitchen tonight. I see families cooking their meals on the barbecue and hear the laughter of our past volunteers as they share food, drink, and stories of their travel adventures. During summer, this area was alive with activity, some people cooking and others diving into the pool just below the terrace, surfacing for a sip of cold beer before sunning themselves on the stone-covered patio encircling the blue-tiled pool.

They came from around the globe, narrating their histories as they watched our glowing sunsets. I often noted how we were more similar than we were different, regardless of age, gender, culture, race, or religion—all of us with dreams and goals, envisioning futures that might come true. Like a slideshow, their faces appear, connecting me to the past and reminding me why we built this place where nothing had flourished.

On weekends, we would open coconuts taken from the many trees around the property and use the white meat and liquid in smoothies. The maracuya plants would overflow with delicious fruit whose delicate flesh would be eaten with a spoon. We would check the mango and avocado plants every season, knowing it might take five years or more to enjoy their gifts. Nevertheless, we would tend to all the fruit trees and gardens on the property's lower level for the simple joy of communing with the earth. Pruning, watering, and weeding became my meditation practice where I could find an inner stillness to nourish me as I nurtured my garden.

Chief puts his head in my lap as if he can sense my uneasiness. Bella wags her tail restlessly and moves up the stairs of an unfinished two-story structure. It's the only building on our property with more than one floor, and we haven't had the funds to finish it. Tonight, the structure stands over the property like a battered sentinel with gaping holes where doors and windows have yet to be installed. Colorless concrete walls enshroud the inner spaces in darkness, a favorite resting place for local bats. Carrying my glass, I follow the dogs to the building. Despite the humidity, I shiver as I enter the bottom floor and turn around.

Surveying this property, built from my tears and sweat, I don't know if I should feel proud of my accomplishment or instead recognize the shackles that bind me to a place where I no longer belong. The question lingers with each sip of aguardiente. I'm standing in a timeless place, between a past that has abandoned me and a future that scares me. Around me, the coconut palms become silhouettes like memories I can no longer recall, buried in the recesses of my mind. It feels so unreal that two years have passed since I first called Ecuador home.

Chief nudges me, insisting I follow him. I follow the dogs up the concrete stairs. I pass the small alcove tucked behind the landing and hidden from view, my refuge when I need to hide. The second floor is empty, the space interrupted only by concrete columns that support the floor and ceiling. I pause on the veranda and look out to the horizon across the dilapidated shacks, fields of withered wild grass, and dead corn stalks that populate this rural village. My chest begins to heave. I cannot reconcile the intelligent, accomplished woman who helps others live their dreams with the woman standing on this cement platform in the middle of the planet. With a deep breath, I release some of the grief I hold clenched in my chest, which has been pried open by the fiery aguardiente swallow by swallow.

Only a few years earlier, I stood under another full moon on the dock outside my Chesapeake Bay apartment and begged for an answer to my question, "Where do I belong?" I prayed for a quieter life, one with meaning and grace. I had a profitable business doing work I enjoyed. I lived in a beautiful spot on the Chesapeake Bay with people who shared their lives with me. My son and his father lived a few minutes away, allowing for frequent visits and shared holidays and birthdays. I had good friends and a life many would envy. Back then, I had what most would term "success." And yet I could not quell the longing in my heart.

From childhood, I'd lived with mystic dreams and visions. They were accepted as ordinary in my family, whose Colombian culture was rooted in the elders' stories about spirits and visitations. Passed from generation to generation, lessons on *anima mundi*—the soul of the world, an intrinsic connection between all living things—permeated the mythologies and fables my parents shared with me at story time. There was no skepticism around unseen forces real enough to move material things, playful spirits that might suddenly cause a door to slam or a lamp to turn on.

Although these experiences seemed normal within my family, the external world had taught me to keep them to myself. I recalled the day in kindergarten at my Catholic school when I told another child I could see spirits. English-speaking children from white, upper-middle-class families had bullied me. I was a dark-skinned, curly-haired little girl who was too skinny to fit into her uniform and spoke only Spanish. I didn't look or sound like anyone they knew. Finally, by mid-year, I had learned enough English to tell my classmate of my "secret powers," hoping to avoid the endless teasing.

That child told the class nun, who was sure I was possessed by a demon. My parents were summoned immediately. I sat contritely in an oversized chair, my Buster Brown shoes dangling in the air outside the Mother Superior's office as my father and mother tried speaking to her in English and then in Spanish. My mother, a wise, beautiful woman whose presence would be felt in any room she entered, came to my defense. In Spanish, she told the nun that I had a vivid imagination and was talking about imaginary friends, a familiar concept to teachers. There were no demons and no need for any kind of exorcism. My parents left with me after the nuns offered understanding smiles and empathetic hand-holding.

That afternoon, I received my first lesson in hiding my access to the unseen world over milk and chocolate chip cookies. "Don't tell the Americans," my mother instructed. She placed the snack on the kitchen table and sat next to me, her favorite apron—the one with drawings of fruits and vegetables—tied around her waist. Gently, she put her hand over mine and explained, "They won't understand. Tell your father or me. But don't tell anyone else."

Confused, I asked my mother, "Did I do something wrong?"

"No, not at all. You have something special, and other people here won't understand it. Remember that small gold cross you wear under your shirt, the one from Colombia? It's like that. You keep your cross and gift hidden because they are precious, but you always carry them wherever you go. Like a special secret that you only share with us. Understand?"

As I remember my mother's words, my hand unconsciously moves to my chest, and I wrap my fingers around the small gold cross that I never take off. She meant to protect me, and following her counsel did that. Adults excused me as a shy and quiet child and later as a loner who didn't quite fit into the extroverted culture of middle school and high school. Books became my escape into alternative realities where I could travel to exotic places and experience historical events without leaving my bedroom. I discovered poetry, finding comfort in how the poet expressed her worldview through rhyme and lyricism. Such an orderly and musical way to describe the unexplainable appealed to me. I felt strangely at home in those undefined spaces, with ease that seemed to come from a memory of belonging to the unknown.

I adapted to the outer world to meet the expectations of a culture that narrowly defined success through money and status. Yet I knew that I was missing a vital piece of myself. Such a yearning to reunite the sacred with the secular hurt my heart, a kind of inconsolable lament that ran silently beyond my life's activities.

In April 2012, I accepted a friend's invitation to Ecuador, never anticipating how this impulsive decision would change my life. There I met a charismatic individual, a shaman, who would entice me to an unexpected journey. Behind his deep, enigmatic eyes, I discerned a potent blend of spirituality, strength, and wisdom.

This encounter occurred at a crucial juncture in my life where I was feeling lost and alone after enduring years of hardship and loss. A devastating divorce following twenty-one years of marriage, the loss of two homes, a painful separation from my son, financial bankruptcy, and the heart-wrenching experience of witnessing my mother's battle with dementia had sapped my courage and resilience.

When I met him, I needed someone to guide me on the spiritual journey I'd always known I would take but had no idea how to begin. I would learn about shamanism, mysticism, and the unseen metaphysical world for the next eight years. I would take a perilous journey to recover the mystery of my soul in the Andean wisdom traditions. However, I never anticipated that I would lose myself in that world. I was resigned, tired, and unaware that I was surrendering my will to this man.

Now, years later, a profound emptiness fills me on this moonlit night between the hills and the ocean, and hope eludes me. My sobbing chokes me. The fears I have forced into a box break through. The aguardiente is merciless. A naked truth blindsides me. I have sold everything I owned and used most of my life's savings to fund my ultimate dream of creating a retreat space for healing. In attempting to merge my sacred and secular worlds, I have forsaken myself for an illusion and handed my soul to a stranger.

An errant mosquito buzzes an insistent scolding in my ear. The muggy air conspires to suffocate me. Images of my past dart back and forth in the corners of the alcove like little nightmares I can't escape.

I collapse from the overwhelming shame I feel at being trapped and deceived. I want to hide not only from him but from everyone, even from the voice in the glass that insists I can survive this. Feeling the burn of the aguardiente in my throat reminds me that I am still alive and resilient. But tonight it isn't enough.

In the moonlight, I fall to my knees and dissolve into a puddle of regret, shame, and self-condemnation. I plead with the moon, "Who do I forgive?" There is no answer, no grand revelation as she bears witness to my breakdown. I become a ball of despair, contracted into a fetal position on the hard concrete floor. I watch as tiny black ants parade over the unfinished floor until, at last, an uneasy sleep overtakes me.

When I wake up, my face is against the cold cement. My clothes are damp from the night's tears and the morning mist. The sun has risen, and Bella has come to cuddle against my body. I squint against the morning light, my eyes feeling the sting from the evening's crying. My hands wander over Bella's smooth fur as she licks my fingers, then my face. I can't help but smile at her innocence, this little being who stayed at my side all night without asking for anything but an affectionate stroke. Slowly, morning enters me as I open my senses to the swaying trees, the songs of the birds, and the salty taste of the sea air that wafts up the hill to my lookout.

I wonder, *Is this what despair feels like? Hopelessness and grief so heavy on the soul that it will crush me?* This place I built as an oasis for healing—mine and others'—is a mirage, like the illusion of life-giving waters in an endless desert on a nomadic journey.

I slowly pull myself up from the floor and stretch my rigid body, unsteady and still feeling the aguardiente's effects. An intense burst of wind hits my face like a slap, demanding that I shake off the evening's lamenting. Light, like crystals, glitters and sparkles on the moist grasses in the valley below. Farm noises—a horse neighing, the rooster crowing, and my neighbor's pig grunting—float up my hill in a cacophony of voices. Still harboring the questions from last night, I hear a new sound in the wind.

As if someone is standing next to me, the voice below the wind whispers into my ear, "There is still hope." I recognize the voice as mine, only different, more melodious, and wiser in its encouragement. As the workers arrive, the same voice commands, "Get up, go. You have work to do." I brush myself off, run my hands over my face and through my damp hair, and call Bella. "Let's go, Bella. We have work to do."

It will be another two years before I rise and save myself.

– 2 –
THE ENCOUNTER

My mother used to say that luck comes in seven-year increments, seven lucky years followed by seven unlucky years. I would say that it all depends on when you start counting.

My seven unlucky years were 2004 to 2011. I experienced so much loss in those seven years that I didn't think I would survive. I remember saying to my friend Judy, "I don't think I can go on. How can I continue?"

Judy is not only one of my dearest friends but also one of the wisest and most authentically spiritual women I know. She is what we call an "old soul." She understands my metaphysical nature. My first overt explorations in spirituality and metaphysics happened in partnership with her. I'd long counted on her advice and valued her perspective.

She didn't answer but instead asked me a series of questions. "What would happen if you lost one more thing?"

"I'd deal with it," I answered.

"And what would happen if something else occurred after that?"

"I'd deal with that too."

"And what would happen if you lost a hundred more things?"

My chest contracted, no longer able to support the idea of such loss. I stopped breathing and instantly felt as if I would die.

My head dropped as I answered softly. "I would stop. I couldn't go on."

She didn't say anything else. That night, a dream confirmed her cryptic answer.

In the dream, two young knights, twins in armor, stood face-to-face wielding their swords. I knew that I was both. Their battle seemed endless, neither of them winning over the other. Soon, the goal of victory was surpassed by the simple desire to stop. Suddenly, one of the knights paused and laid down his sword. Kneeling in front of the other, he bowed and surrendered. The other knight pulled him to his feet and embraced him, and they merged, becoming one whole person. I woke up.

This dream showed me my answer. I had to stop fighting and surrender all my ideas of how my life was supposed to be so I could have the life I was meant to have. In that moment of clarity, every loss became a gift, eliminating what did not serve me on my journey. This hard-won understanding was both enlightening and painful.

The walls of my bedroom seemed to contract as I sat up. My space became small and suffocating. I rose from the bed, put on my fluffy white robe and terry cloth slippers, and left the apartment with Finn, my British golden retriever, who had been sleeping in the alcove. Finn had come with me to this place by the Chesapeake Bay after my separation. Navigating the outdoor spiral stairs of my tiny apartment, I followed the sound of the tide lapping at the stones by the pier. At the water's edge, I dropped to my knees and sobbed. Being all white, Finn shone through the darkness like an angel comforting me with his presence. The salty spray from the water moistened my face like holy water sprinkled on a penitent. At that moment, I accepted the invitation to a deeper life without judging the one I was living. I felt a kind of grace and freedom in giving over to what I didn't know but trusted.

I sat on one of the stone benches with Finn until the sun slowly rose, a soft glow on the horizon morphing into gold, red, and orange ribbons streaking across the sky. Finn nudged me. I put my arms around him and wiped the droplets that had anointed my face. We then walked carefully up the slippery lawn and climbed the staircase to the place that had become my sanctuary.

My journey to Ecuador starts in 2006 when my friend Megan introduces me to Carlos Luna, a traditional Ecuadorian shaman. She is one of the few friends who knows of my metaphysical experiences. She encourages me to share them with Carlos, explaining that he could help me understand them.

"Who is he?" I ask Megan when she first mentions him during a walk on the B&A Trail through Severna Park.

"I met him in DC, and we've been dating. It's gotten serious. He's a deeply spiritual man, and he's from Ecuador. He's a psychologist and a shaman," she explains matter-of-factly as she stoops to tie her sneaker. I wait for a moment, and as she stands, she adds, "He has explained so much to me about my work as a transpersonal psychologist that has opened my eyes to new ways to deal with trauma."

"I don't know what that means, Megan. Is he some kind of priest or medicine man?" I'm curious but wary since Megan has been in other relationships that have not turned out well.

"Not quite. Shamans are wisdom keepers for their tribes and society. They're healers. The difference between them and traditional healers is that they heal the soul. They can do that because they interact with the spirit world. Carlos comes from a lineage of shamans going back six generations. He's the real thing, Alicia, and I know he can help you understand your past extraordinary experiences and maybe help you develop that intuition you have."

I hesitatingly agree to meet him. "Okay, Megan. I'll talk to him, but honestly, I'm not sure what difference it will make."

"You'll see," she says cheerfully, taking my arm. "Come to the house tomorrow afternoon. I'll let him know you're coming. I've already told him about you."

"It's a date!" I say, hiding my doubt behind our laughter.

After my walk with Megan, I return home and scan the Internet for information on shamans and shamanism. I find photos of Indigenous men dressed in caps or headdresses, mostly Peruvian or Amazonian, blowing smoke and drinking ayahuasca. I read a few articles that further confuse me. When I arrive at our meeting, doubt is heavy on my mind, like a blanket. Nevertheless, I still hope he might explain this lifelong sensation of being different and, as I would half-jokingly say, dropped off on the wrong planet.

I enter the house through the side door into the kitchen. Megan is making tea and has placed a plate of cookies on the kitchen table. "Hey, so glad you came!" she says excitedly. "He'll be right here."

A few minutes later, Carlos appears in the doorway. He seems to fill the opening. "Hola, Meganita," he says, hugging Megan. "Is this your friend?"

"Yes. Alicia, meet Carlos. Carlos, this is Alicia. Her parents were Colombian, so she speaks Spanish too. I'm sure you'll have lots to talk about." Megan sets two cups of chamomile tea on the table. "I'm going for a run. I'll see you later." Then, after kissing Carlos's cheek, she leaves through the side door.

Turning to me, he says in a heavy Latin accent, "I am so happy to meet you." Carlos moves deliberately, as if each step and each turn of his body were planned. Even the air surrounding him seems to flow around his movement. "Please sit down, Alicia." He motions to the chair at the table under the window.

I keep my eyes on him as I turn toward the chair. He's a thick man, not very tall, with a colorful bandana holding back his long, graying hair. A full mustache punctuates his broad, tanned face. A necklace made of tiny shells and beads, with several puma teeth, gives him a formidable appearance. Rings of turquoise, silver, and lapis lazuli embellish his hands, and a colorful tagua bracelet adorns his wrist. I notice that he wears an embroidered guayabera, a traditional South American cotton shirt for men, typically worn loose. He wears it neatly tucked into his jeans—a fondness for food shows through the shirt, which tightly hugs his torso.

Sensing my uneasiness, he moves the plate of cookies close to me. "Megan made these. I love chocolate chips," he pronounces. His eyes sparkle like a child's as he slowly puts one into his mouth, savoring the melting chips on his tongue. I can't help but smile at his delight with the still-warm cookies.

So, this is a shaman? I think. All images of headdresses and blowing smoke disappear as I watch this paradox of a man in front of me. I can see how he could be an imposing figure. It isn't the person but the energy around him that comes across as direct and enveloping me. I am sensitive to how energy flows between all living things, lessons I learned from my ancestors and my parents. I am watching a masterful conductor and, at the same time, a trickster or magician. Alarms go off in my head even as his smile invites me to open up to him.

I sit down with Carlos at the kitchen table and take a cookie. I sip tea as he pulls back his chair, sits down, and eats another cookie. His eyes are both smiling and piercing, as if he can read my mind and is enjoying the story he discovers.

"Well," I begin, "as Megan told you, my parents are Colombian. I was born in the United States a year after they moved here. My father insisted that we live as Colombians, so we spoke Spanish at home, learned all the myths of our culture, and danced *cumbia* in the living room every Sunday. One of the things that made me feel different than people here is that we would have certain experiences that were normal to us but not normal to others. My mother told me not to tell anyone, and I told only a few people. Megan is one of those people. She didn't think I was crazy."

By now, he is focused on me, listening with curiosity as he evaluates my story. "What kind of experiences did you have? Were they visions, dreams, voices, or simply knowing something you didn't know you knew?"

"Depends. All of the above," I answer. Gradually, I begin to tell him of my experiences and the things that happened in our house, which my parents interpreted as visitations from friends and ancestors.

I pause. "Does any of this make any sense to you? Megan says you're a shaman, and you can help me understand these experiences and even develop my intuition more. But I don't really understand what shamanism is. Can you explain this to me?"

Carlos spreads his hands and arms on the table, reaching toward me. "Shamanism is the oldest wisdom tradition in the world. It is based on a *cosmovisión*, or a cosmic worldview, that incorporates the earth, matter, cosmos, and spirit. Each is real and part of what makes us human and spiritual." He pauses before continuing. "In our tradition, everything has a life force that emanates from the soul. We are all brothers and sisters with the earth and all living beings. We all come from the same place," he states, wiping a bit of chocolate from his cheek.

Strangely, this makes sense even though my mind keeps telling me it sounds like New Age woo-woo. I can't deny that his words feel like a truth I know but mistrust. "Then why don't more people know about it?" I ask, my skepticism seeping out of my words. I recall all the New Age gurus barking their miracles at the lonely crowds of seekers hoping for redemption. *That's not me*, I think. I begin strategizing how to leave gracefully without hurting his feelings.

I notice a flick of Carlos's eyes, as if he senses my doubt. He turns his gaze toward the window, searching the trees for an answer. Sighing, he continues. "Humans have forgotten our connection with the Creator. Instead, we choose materialistic things and lives of productivity over the simplicity of the natural world and the rhythms of creation."

As I listen to him speak of this connection, I recall the sensation of being in my kayak on the Chesapeake Bay. I long for the freedom and openness that only nature can provide. Paddling always feels like communion with life, a merging that ebbs and flows like the waters of the bay, a rhythm that moves me deeper into my body and soul.

Carlos rises from the table and slowly moves to the kitchen sink for a glass of water. He pauses to wipe the counter before returning to the table and our conversation. "For shamans, the unseen world is as real as the seen world. We easily access both at any moment. Everything is filtered through the wisdom passed down from generation to generation. I am a sixth-generation shaman. The shaman's role is to serve our community using that wisdom for healing the mind, body, and, most importantly, the soul." Then, chuckling and making a dramatic sweeping movement with his arms, he adds, "We are the doctors of the soul."

I smile at his drama, but I'm not convinced anyone can heal a soul. It's not that I don't believe in miracles; I do. But I have become jaded by all the false teachers, the influential New Age gurus, and the existential promises of enlightenment from so-called spiritual practices. At the same time, I can sense a crack in my skepticism driven by a longing to find a truth that I know exists but don't know how to access. Is it possible that this man with a childlike quality in a bearlike body could be the one to reveal the elusive road to my unanswered questions?

Carlos's eyes shift from a passive softness to a sharp intensity focused on my face, as if he were excavating my memories. Something inside me surrenders, a bursting of unfulfilled questions and the fear that I might lose my only chance at answers. On faith, I confide to him a lifetime of experiences from childhood to the current moment. Like a flood, they come forth, one after the other. These are stories I have not told anyone. I sense that only by revealing these experiences to Carlos could he possibly help me understand them. He occasionally comments, punctuating his remarks with a smile or a joke to lighten the mood.

I am falling into his voice, a melodic tone that mesmerizes me and anesthetizes my resistance to sharing what had been buried. We are somewhere else, out of time, having this conversation like two old friends who have not seen each other for many years. Between questions, we laugh out loud and eat more cookies. An unusual affection is unexpectedly growing in my heart. With a surprising cadence and tone, Carlos's voice lulls me into a deep sense of safety. As I become more comfortable, more memories arise, and I share them with him. Slowly something unfolds within me, hurting like the ache of a fist that has been closed tightly, then finally opens to free and stretch the ligaments.

I confess, "I've never told anyone these things, and honestly, I don't know why I'm telling you."

He pushes his chair around the table so he's closer to me and reaches for me. His thick fingers encircle my hands, now cupped together tightly, as I hold back tears.

"*Yo sé*," he acknowledges. "That is why we are the doctors of the soul. *Dios te bendiga*." His voice softens with the blessing.

The wind has picked up outside, jostling the branches of the trees nearest the house. The frilly kitchen curtain blows into the room as if waving to us in slow motion. I haven't noticed any movement in the room until this moment, aside from Carlos and I and the ebb and flow of our conversation. The breeze makes the hair on my arms stand up, a momentary chill bringing me into my body. The scent of lilacs catches me by surprise. I fidget, feeling the stiff wooden chair against my lower back. He is talking, but I can't hear him any longer. As if it's underwater, the room seems to blur and his voice becomes an echo of sounds I don't recognize. It isn't drowsiness, although at first it feels like that. I imagine being in a fishbowl, swimming and looking at the outer world with fascination while feeling safe and secure in my little enclosure. My tiny fish mouth spews bubbles. Am I still talking? Yes, I can see myself through the glass fishbowl, back in the kitchen, talking to Carlos, sharing more of my history and asking him questions I've held on to for so long.

A strong gust of wind charges through the open window, pushing a small ceramic vase over the sill. Before we can move, it crashes to the floor, breaking into pieces under the table. The sharp sound breaks my trance, a kind of surfacing from the waters that had held me moments ago. Suddenly I feel alert, not in a nervous way, but energized. The heaviness I carried in my body is replaced by an inner expansiveness, as if I have left the fishbowl's confinement and entered the immense ocean.

Carlos is already under the table, sweeping the shards from the vase into a dustpan. With surprising agility, he lifts himself from the floor and empties it into the trash. Then he turns to me, asking, "How was your swim?"

For a moment, I stop breathing and can't answer. My face must have registered surprise. He smiles and, from the other side of the room, asks again, "How was your swim?"

"It was great," I awkwardly answer, stunned by the question. I take a deep breath. "Why are you asking me that?"

He wipes his hands on the dishcloth by the sink. Approaching the table, he scans my face as he sits down. "Your memories confuse you, but at the same time, they keep you safe. If you don't know the answers to your questions, you do not have to take responsibility for the direction of your life. That keeps you in a tiny bowl when you could be swimming in the ocean."

I take another deep breath but say nothing. So many questions run through my mind. How can he know what my imagination is showing me? Where did I go during our conversation? Peering out the window, I hear the birds singing, now hidden in the shadows of the branches as evening approaches. Where did the time go?

For a moment, Carlos becomes serious. He leans back in his chair as he extends his arms toward me. He reaches for my hands and again cups them in his. "Alicia, if you had been born into our tribe ages ago, your gifts would've been recognized and nurtured. But in this culture, no one accepts other realities that cannot be seen or explained but only felt with the heart. I invite you to explore this unseen world with me. I can help you better understand who you are and how to serve others without hurting yourself."

I feel a ribbon of warmth from his hands flowing up my arms and into my chest. The image of a sunflower bursting open in my heart space appears. Suddenly, all rationalizations, the need for proof, and any confusion or doubt dissipate. "Yes, I would like that," I say softly, fighting back tears. Carlos stands, pulls me to my feet, and wraps his burly arms around me as I bury my face in his chest. I'm not sure how long we stand there together. I pull my face back and notice that the sun has set and fireflies have appeared in the garden. I take that as a sign that this is the next step on my journey.

When Megan returns, she finds an empty plate and two old friends laughing and joking in Spanish. "Well, I see you got along and liked the cookies," she says with a knowing smile. "I ran some errands and had a great run. So, what did you decide?"

Carlos and I glance at each other, and he answers. "*Es valiente. Es guerrera.*" She is brave. She is a warrior. "I will help her understand her heritage and gifts. *Sí?*"

"*Sí,*" I answer with a weak smile. I am suddenly tired, spent from sharing so much of my history, which I've hidden since the day my mother told me not to tell anyone. So many times in my life, I've questioned what is real and what is my imagination. Today feels real, and Carlos's question—"How was your swim?"—convinces me I've made a connection in some liminal space I can visit again if I surrender to the possibility that there is more to life (and myself) than I am aware of.

After that meeting, I become Carlos's client and student. My work with him becomes a salve for the unexplained longing I have felt all my life. In the six years I work with him, I come to care for him as a brother. Both my extrasensory experiences and my intuition blossom, and my desire for a deeper understanding of the spiritual world takes me to Ecuador and to another shaman, the one who will transform me into a spiritual warrior.

− 3 −
ECUADOR

When Megan and Carlos invited me to Ecuador, I had already been working with Carlos for several years. I was also recovering from finalizing my divorce in January 2012 after a two-year separation, and I was leaving my son with his father as part of the agreement. The pain of stepping out the door knowing I would never return as the wife or the mother who makes her son's daily breakfast broke me. I buried my grief in an imaginary coffin in the woods of the Chesapeake Bay, where I went to live. The need to survive my heartbreak and the truth that life must go on deflected any chance at another relationship. I had put my heart on hold and distracted myself with my work. It never occurred to me to look for love. I was simply trying to rebuild my life.

There are times when a quick decision changes the direction of your life. Like going down a street you're curious about but have never traveled, you enter with a sense of anticipation of what you might find. Nothing prepares you for the reality waiting for you at the end of the road.

It was like that when I accepted Carlos's invitation to visit Ecuador and stay at his home in Quito, where he lived during annual trips to his home country. We agreed that I would help Megan with her thesis about shamanism and trauma. Carlos's older brother, a powerful Ecuadorian shaman, lived nearby. He was Megan's mentor, and I would translate for him. Imagining that a new adventure and culture would renew my energy made it easy to say yes. After working with Carlos for years and knowing Megan for a long time, I trusted they would take care of me. The opportunity to learn more about shamanism and Andean wisdom traditions also piqued my curiosity.

I arrive in Quito on April 11, 2012, close to midnight. The airport is just beyond the city, making landing a nerve-racking experience. We are so tight on approach that I can see the balconies of apartment buildings. The plane is packed; cramped seats and stale air make me unsteady. As we touch down, Ecuadorian passengers stand up to bring their luggage down from the overhead compartments, ignoring the repeated warnings to stay seated. Pushing and shoving each other, they drag their luggage down the aisle while I remain seated, patiently waiting for them to pass. I am the last to leave the plane despite only having a backpack.

After going through customs, I follow the crowd to the large, open room where our luggage has been dumped. I wonder if my bags have arrived and question the wisdom of choosing an inconspicuous black suitcase that blends into the hundreds of others on the floor. My brain is foggy after hours of flying through the night, so I don't notice Megan and Carlos walking toward me until they are at my side. They welcome me with a hug, and we begin searching for my suitcase. I sense that someone is watching me, that intuitive feeling that makes the back of your neck tingle. I look toward the door and spot a short man with wavy black hair peeking out from under a baseball cap that hides his eyes. I intuitively recognize Carlos's older brother, Bolivar Napoleon, or Napo, as his friends call him, a man Carlos considers a mentor and father figure.

After retrieving my luggage, we approach him and I greet him in Spanish. I spontaneously hug him and immediately feel a surge of energy, like an electrical current going through my body. I instinctively pull back, look into his dark eyes, and blurt out, "I feel like I've known you my whole life."

He replies softly, "*Bienvenida a Ecuador, Alicia.*" Welcome to Ecuador, Alicia.

Years later, Napo will tell me that he felt the same surge of energy when we embraced. *This isn't supposed to happen*, he told himself. Nevertheless, it was his first clue to our destined encounter, which he did not expect but had perceived in his visions.

That evening we take a taxi back to Carlos's house in Quito, stuffing ourselves and the luggage into the van's three bench seats. After lugging my bags to the third-floor bedroom where I will be staying, we gather in the kitchen, and Megan opens a bottle of wine. After an hour of conversation, I am overcome with fatigue. I say good night and go up the tiled outdoor stairs to a small room on the upper terrace. This room will be my home for the next ten days. A twin-size bed covered with colorful wool blankets greets me. The dim light obscures the decor. I barely get into my pajamas before falling asleep. I have traveled far, yet little do I know that my journey is just beginning.

The following day, I wake to the sounds of light rain. I huddle in my blankets, thankful for my flannel pajamas. They keep me warm and comfortable. The stiffness in my body from the night before has lessened during the night. I stretch out only to discover that my feet hang over the edge of the bed. I suppose beds in Ecuador are meant for shorter people. The room comes into focus as slivers of light penetrate the cloth curtain hanging over a small window.

I ease into the day, balanced precariously between a luscious dream state and the morning's chill. The scent of sage catches my attention. Wrapping a blanket around myself, I step onto a rough rug at the side of the bed. Sniffing around the room brings me to a small painted cupboard in the corner. It creaks as I open it, the door unsure on its hinges. Inside, I find several bundles of sage and what

I later learn is palo santo, a native wood that is burned in shamanic ceremonies. Small pots of herbs line the shelves, and tiny porcelain figures—a jaguar, tiger, rabbit, and fish—are tucked into one of the open spaces where a drawer has fallen off. On the upper shelf is a bottle, like a Coca-Cola bottle, filled with a dark, greenish liquid and herbs. A white ribbon, crinkled and stained, encircles the bottleneck. A cork keeps the bottle closed. I am tempted to open it but change my mind. A rattle made from a gourd, with leather ties and engraved symbols, lies on a red felt cloth next to a painted ocarina. I put the ocarina to my lips and blow. It makes a pleasing musical sound that changes when I move my fingers over the holes in the shell. I set it down with the vibration of the notes still ringing in my ears.

Now done with the cupboard, I close the door and look around the room. Simple decor makes it comfortable and inviting. A small, old-fashioned lamp that looks like a gas light with a frosted glass top sits intentionally on a white knit doily that is placed on a round tea table. The room is decorated in Andean art, and colorful textiles—the rug, wool blanket, and a woven shawl—bring back memories of my travels to Colombia with my mother when I was younger. Although I have never been here, there is something familiar about my room. Perhaps the calming scent of sage or textiles like those I had at home make me feel safe.

I shuffle back to the bed and cocoon in the blankets. I feel the cool, damp air on my face. The Quiteños say that every day holds all four seasons. I was warned it might be warm and sunny one minute and a soaking downpour the next.

A knock on the door forces me out of my cozy bed. Opening the door, I see Megan's smiling face. "Get up, Alicia. We have coffee and breakfast all ready." Suddenly, I feel my belly yawning for food.

"Coffee!" I exclaim as she descends the stairs laughing.

There is no bathroom on the terrace level, only this tiny bedroom, an afterthought to the rest of the house. Wrapping myself in a robe I find draped over a chair, I carefully climb down the outdoor tile stairs, slippery from an early morning drizzle, and knock at the front door.

Carlos greets me with a big smile. "Shower?" I ask. He motions toward the bathroom, a cramped space with a small tiled shower, sink, and toilet. That's when I discover that his house has no hot water. The shock of the cold shower wakes me. I swear quietly, rebelling against the confining shower stall and the burst of icy water. Recovering, I dry myself off, get back into my warm pajamas and robe, and carefully head back up the staircase, which is now drying in the equatorial sun's rays, which have burst from behind the clouds. Rummaging through my suitcase, I pull out my black leggings, a long-sleeved T-shirt, and an old college sweatshirt before stepping into my socks and sneakers. In less than thirty minutes, I am ready to meet the day and desperately need coffee.

The kitchen is a small space that has a low ceiling and is tucked into the back of the house. It is simple, just a small table and four chairs, a counter holding the sink and assorted cooking items, dark wood cupboards, a refrigerator, and a stove. I notice mismatched tiles around the sink, as if someone had taken the wrong puzzle pieces and concocted a collage of colors and patterns. A window over the table looks out onto the building next door. I drink in the smell of newly brewed coffee, anticipating the pungency of Ecuador's morning beverage. Being of Colombian descent, I have a deep appreciation for coffee. My ex-husband used to say that my coffee was so strong my spoon saluted when I put it into the mug. I hope this morning's cup will match that.

Carlos and Napo are already at the table eating the freshly baked rolls Napo brought from the neighborhood bakery. They drink tea, but Megan knows I prefer coffee and sets a large cup of java in front of me as soon as I take my place at the table. The bun melts in my mouth. Each bite is a light, buttery gift that complements the coffee's intensity. Between mouthfuls and sips, I join the morning conversation about where they will take me today. I'm ready for anything, and given that I don't know what to expect, I'm happy to follow along.

"How did you sleep?" asks Napo.

"I slept very well, thank you." We speak in Spanish. The conversation is animated. They are excited about showing me around Quito and sharing their world with me.

I watch Napo as he chats with his brother. Napo surprises me with his charisma and sense of humor. The night before, he had appeared shy and a bit aloof. This morning, his eyes sparkle like diamonds in a deep well. The affection the brothers share is evident in the ease with which they banter.

Listening to Carlos and Napo, I am thankful my immigrant parents chose to speak Spanish at home. My parents shared their Colombian heritage with their children—food, music, customs, and photos from their lives in Colombia—all of which made my ancestry come alive and filled me with love for a country that means so much to me. The Latin beat playing in the background as I eat breakfast flows through my veins and makes me recall dancing with my father in the living room when I was a small child.

My father had been strict. He had not allowed us to speak English in the house, saying we would learn it "out there." He would say, "In our house, we are Colombian, and Colombians speak Spanish." Although it was annoying at the time, I am particularly grateful today. Because of my father, I developed an ability with languages and a curiosity about other cultures.

I studied in France and Mexico during college, and I also spent years traveling the world. Languages come quickly to me. I appreciate that each has its unique music and poetry. Being multilingual allows me to enter other cultures and fosters an appreciation for their uniqueness and differences. As I explore my own identity, being exposed to other countries always feels like an adventure into each nation's stories. No longer in my comfort zone, holding on to what might be familiar, I open myself up to those unlike me and find the gifts in others. My beliefs and assumptions are constantly challenged as I unearth unexpected aspects of myself that have been hidden by society's conditioning. Seeing myself reflected in others is how I make meaning of my life.

On my first morning in Ecuador, we decide to go to Quito by bus. It is easy and cheap. This will be my first experience with the city buses. We walk a few blocks to the bus stop, which is now busy with locals on their way to the city center.

"Alicia, keep your money and camera inside your coat. Buses are crowded, and at any moment, you will be pickpocketed," warns Carlos.

A bus spattered with half-torn advertisements and smelling of gas fumes lumbers toward us, abruptly stopping beyond our spot. Grabbing my hand, Napo pushes me into the bus as Carlos does the same to Megan. We squeeze into the crowd as the bus starts with a jolt, sending passengers flying against each other like dolls. Bodies press into one another as we all shift in unison, trying not to fall into someone's lap. The lucky ones capture the few empty seats. Napo snatches a spot for me, then stands over me protectively as we ride to the city center. His eyes scan the people around us, searching out any potential threats. He reminds me of a panther, his body wound up and tight, as if he were preparing to move swiftly should any danger appear. I'm conflicted about his hovering. I'm unsure if I should feel grateful for his vigilance or annoyed at his possessiveness.

The noxious fumes fill my nostrils, mixing with the heavy perfume worn by the woman in the fake fur coat who sits in the seat ahead of me. Several people speak loudly into their phones, competing with the honking horns of the cars in traffic beside us. The bus weaves dangerously between cars as we head toward the center of Quito.

After thirty minutes of being stepped on and pushed in my seat, Napo leans down and yells in my ear, "Now! Get up now! We are here." He pulls me up, pushes me toward the door, and exits ahead of me.

Before I can get down, the bus starts moving again. I jump, and Napo catches me as my feet land on the street.

"Well, that was an adventure," I say, laughing.

"Now you are Ecuadorian," Napo says, smiling. "You survived your first bus trip."

Carlos sets a plan for the day—our stops and what they want me to see. "Alicia, you can't just go off on your own without telling anyone when something catches your attention," he says sternly. "You must stay near us. There are many pickpockets, and the cars here will run you over without a second thought when crossing the street." He then assigns Napo to be my protector and guide.

"Sure, Carlos," I answer, knowing this warning will not hinder my exploration. I am well traveled, speak Spanish, blend in, and have an insatiable curiosity that will lead me wherever I need to go, bodyguard or not. Today is the first day of my adventure, and I enjoy it to the fullest.

Quito does not match my idea of a city in a developing country. We are met by tall buildings—not quite skyscrapers but elegant, contemporary towers of glass and steel lining busy, loud streets. I am surprised at how cosmopolitan the city is. It has museums, galleries, restaurants, malls, and everything you would find in most international cities. Quito is the capital of Ecuador, with over two million inhabitants. It rises to an elevation of 9,350 feet in the Andes Mountains. Its central square is located about one kilometer from zero latitude. The Ecuadorians joke about the effects of being in *la mitad del mundo*, the middle of the earth. They attribute their laissez-faire attitude and forgetfulness to what they call "attitude zero." It is a great excuse to take days off or conveniently forget deadlines. I admit to experiencing brain fog while there, which my hosts claim is a symptom of attitude zero. I assume it is the altitude or my response to having no worries or cares, something I am not accustomed to and heartily welcome.

We start our tour at the Plaza de San Francisco, where a church by the same name towers over the square. Men and women of all ages and attires sit or stroll around the plaza. They visit with one another, admire the architecture, and people-watch. Towering over the plaza from the nearby hill is *La Virgen del Panecillo*, a 135-foot-tall statue made of seven thousand aluminum pieces. In classic Madonna iconography, the figure depicts a winged woman standing on a globe and stepping on a snake. It can be seen from any location in the city and is named after the hill's shape, which resembles a type of small bread. All Quiteños have prayed to the virgin at some time in their lives.

We visit several other churches, not as large but equally beautiful with their stained glass and sacred icons peering out from the numerous alcoves. As is my tradition, I light a candle in each church, saying a simple prayer of thanks or making a plea to watch over me and my loved ones.

As I walk the city's hills, my lungs begin to constrict. I keep stopping to breathe. I scold myself for not working out more until I remember Quito's elevation. I have lived most of my life at sea level, so the altitude is taking a toll.

As lunchtime approaches, we walk on cobblestone streets, admiring colonial architecture and searching for a place to eat. A musician seated in front of the fountain plays an upbeat melody on his guitar. He is surrounded by a flock of doves, an audience of feathered fans. Children dance around him, tossing breadcrumbs on the stone walkway. My nostrils awaken to the smell of spicy cooking down a small alley away from the plaza.

Few things are as sacred to Ecuadorians as food—except maybe soccer. Carlos and Napo search for food as if an internal alarm clock has gone off. Finally, we stop at a cramped one-room restaurant with not more than ten tables covered in dime-store plastic tablecloths. We enter from the street through a low archway, a typical type of doorway in the area's old buildings. They order *almuerzo*, the meal of the day, without looking at the menu.

Carlos and Napo tease me, knowing that my taste runs to more eclectic fare. "Alicia is having her first real Ecuadorian meal today!" They know my eating style is organic, with small portions and beautifully presented food. These plates overflow their edges and are heavy on starch and meat.

They continue, "How is your day so far? What do you like about Ecuador?"

I join in the fun, replying, "Okay, guys, I'm happy to let you be the tour guides for this adventure. And I'm hungry! The restaurant smells like good food, and I'll admit, it's so rare to have a home-cooked meal at a restaurant."

I spy three women cooking behind a bamboo curtain, and the enticing aromas of a humble but well-run kitchen escape from the small room in back. I hadn't realized my hunger until I sat down, anticipating this new culinary experience.

With pride and a big smile, one of the women serves me a large bowl of chicken soup, a light broth with a touch of cilantro and hunks of yucca, bits of vegetables, and a chicken thigh swimming provocatively in the broth. I'm full by the time I finish it, but this is only the first course. Silence falls over the table as munching and sipping sounds replace conversation. The main course is a *seco de pollo*, braised chicken, accompanied by the ever-present plantains and rice. Fresh juice of *tomate de arbol* (a fruit from the Sierra) and a flan-like dessert follow the entrée. The older woman who served us takes our dishes and asks if we enjoyed the food. We are effusive in our approval, and she leaves smiling broadly, excitedly telling the others that her visitors are pleased. Finally, we shuffle out of the restaurant, content, satiated, and ready for more walking.

Napo and I chat about my trip and our lives. He surprises me when he protectively takes my arm as we cross the street. There is such a stark contrast between the people here who stroll arm in arm, engaged with one another, and what I am used to in the United States, where people walk focused on their destination, their eyes never meeting and their bodies never touching.

"I've never been to the United States," Napo proudly states.

"Would you ever want to visit?" I ask.

"My brother is there. I might visit him one day, but I don't think I'd like life there. It's too hectic, and people live separated from the Creator. I have seen American movies, making me think I would not like it there. I don't understand that culture." I sense a wariness behind his words and wonder if he'll ever make it to the States. If he came, he might change his mind about Americans.

After lunch, we come upon an international photography exhibit. A woman is being filmed while she reports on the exhibition, which has not yet opened to the public. Carlos approaches her and asks if we can enter early. He waves his hands around with a big smile on his face as he makes her laugh, and—surprisingly—he charms her into letting us enter. After a few minutes, he motions for us to come in. She allows us to enter on the condition that we stay away from the film crew.

This exhibit is not what I expected. Rows and rows of photographs depicting natural and manufactured disasters, war, and famine explode in black and white, each image measuring at least one meter by one meter. My chest clenches as I walk from one photo to another, and I fight to hide the tears that arise. I feel like a voyeur, a secret witness to the suffering of humans I will never know. Through the photos, my humanity intertwines with theirs. Seeing the suffering humans can inflict on each other, and the planet, is heartbreaking. My heart feels as if it will explode. I hide in a nearby stairwell that is partially hidden from the main room. Like a dam bursting, my tears flow as I rummage in my daypack for tissues.

These photographs of devastation, faces with haunted eyes, children crying, and women staring blankly, numb from loss, find a foothold deep inside me, as if I've been shown a history of the world's darkness. How do I hold all that with compassion and grace when everything in me screams, *Run!*? I needed to find a transcendent response to balance suffering with meaning in the face of this desolation.

Napo is watching me. I won't learn this until later, but he keeps his eyes on me from a distance, as if he's inquiring into what those devastating photographs make me feel. He slowly approaches me as I rest on the stairs, gathering myself and breathing to gain composure. He sits next to me and silently holds my hand. I'm not sure how long we stay there, but his presence calms me without intruding on my internal conversation about human suffering.

This is holy ground, this place of witnessing, allowing tears to mingle with prayers—an ordinary life made sacred in a damp stairwell in the middle of the world, held gently by a wisdom keeper.

I won't realize it until years later, but my connection with Napo is born in silence, unlike my past relationships, where I was more concerned with what we did, where we went, or what activities interested us. Being with Napo is novel, and it begins by inhabiting my life unconventionally. Without the extreme conditions of my regular life distracting me from my feelings and sensations, I slowly become present to my truth. Ecuador creates a sequence of moments, like stepping stones in a river taking me to the other side, where a new life is forming.

But now it is late afternoon and time to return to Calderon, the area on the north side of Quito where the brothers live. We arrive as evening falls. Napo never mentions my tears. After a light meal at Carlos's house, Napo goes home—he lives only a few doors down from his brother. I say good night and climb to my room, eager for quiet time to reflect on my experience and write in my journal.

This first day in Ecuador begins a chain of events I could never have imagined. With each passing day, the possibility of living in a different way enters my awareness. When we hike to waterfalls, share a meal with family, or converse with traditional artisans, I learn to connect to others and myself through my heart instead of my intellect. Slowly, I begin feeling safe enough to open myself to the flow of life. Each day makes me more aware of the chasm between the life I was attached to and a life I can only imagine. This tug-of-war will go on for years as I peel away layers and shed old beliefs, assumptions, and judgments. Finally, I will meet a black hole, a void in my universe daring me to birth someone new. Then I will set off on an eight-year journey to the life that awaits me on the other side.

— 4 —
THE LESSON AT PEGUCHE

As the days fly by, Napo and I grow closer. Our conversations last into the wee hours of the night. I feel I have discovered a genuine witness who understands my essential nature and can help me navigate my spiritual journey. I have never had conversations like these with anyone. The intensity of our conversations grows as they become more profound.

Napo is a paradox. He exudes a harmony of masculine and feminine energy balanced in a way I have never encountered in another human being. We sit in the living room one evening as Megan and Carlos cook dinner. I recline against the sofa arm with my legs across his lap. His hands rest on my legs. During the pause in our conversation, my eyes fixate on his hands. Although his hands are not large, his fingers are long and elegant. His skin is dark and youthful, belying his age. I turn his hand over in mine, then cup it between my palms.

"Your hands are so feminine and delicate, Napo," I remark. "They are not the hands of most men, hands that are usually rough and thick."

He looks surprised, and I misinterpret his expression for a moment.

"I'm sorry. I didn't mean to offend you. On the contrary, I love your hands. Something about their shape and feel is healing to me."

Looking directly into my eyes, he says, "No one has ever noticed my feminine nature as you sense it. For a shaman, this feminine energy is essential to our connection to the Creator."

He goes on to explain that for a shaman, this means power. "The feminine is the life-giving force of all creation. The masculine is the active energy that directs and manifests in the material world that which craves to be born."

In his words, I recognize my desire to balance feminine and masculine energy, to transcend a predominantly patriarchal and destructive culture.

"Alicia, we are all both feminine and masculine," he explains. "We exist as a collaboration between a male sperm and a female egg. We bring both our mother and our father into our being. Structurally, we are bisexual even if we do not have an identity as bisexual. Men fear their feminine structure, becoming homophobic when the feminine arises in them or another. Women are more apt to embrace their masculine side because of the strong feminine."

I shift to a sitting position. With my hand on his lap, we both lean back. The couch welcomes our bodies, wrapping us softly in its cushions as he continues his lesson.

"Women as the womb hold the essence of life within them, but they don't understand their power. Women do not understand that patriarchy attempts to oppress this force because men fear they will lose their masculinity. They are unaware that the feminine exists in them as well."

He continues, "To be fully integrated is to unify the masculine and feminine aspects. There are three aspects required for unity. First, there are the elements in the body or somatically that we call our gender. Second, there is the genetic material of both our mother and father that exists in our blood. And third, the images we construct about what it means to be masculine and feminine influence how we embody that balance in life. When you understand that these are the influences from within and externally, and you pay attention to how they exist in you, then you are ready to embrace the feminine and masculine within yourself, and that is power."

Napo's words often enter me softly, just as they do at this moment. Like a deep breath, the concepts of masculine and feminine find a place of knowing within me. I do not need mental machinations or rationalizations. Instead, there is an instant acknowledgment, as if he has jarred awake a memory deeply embedded in my psyche.

We sit quietly for a few minutes, holding hands, simultaneously together and in our own worlds. Then Carlos enters the room and stops as if he senses the depth of our conversation. He stands in the doorway for a full minute before donning a broad smile and announcing dinner, waving us into the kitchen where wine and spaghetti await.

I will later learn that Napo's power as a shaman is kept in check by the frailties of his human condition and his difficult childhood. I'll discover that he is indeed an unpredictable paradox. He can be as joyful as a child and as dark as an eclipse, as kind and nurturing as a mother to her child and as brutal and destructive as any force of nature. Nothing is ever what it seems with him. In time, I will discover that the brilliant light in his soul can abruptly turn into a deep, foreboding darkness.

I see a glimpse of this paradox halfway through my trip. Napo, Carlos, Megan, and I take a bus to Otavalo to visit a family Carlos and Napo adopted and have helped for years. The family patriarch had also been a shaman, and Carlos and Napo promised to care for his family after he died. True to their word, they visit Otavalo regularly, bringing food and supplies. My excitement about spending a few days in a hotel with hot water and good Internet almost matches my anticipation for meeting their adopted family.

The bus ride to Otavalo takes two hours, weaving through the Andes north of Quito. The green landscape reminds me of the summer I spent in Colombia with my mother when I was ten years old. The winding curves reveal one stunning vista after another until the Imbabura volcano comes into view, hovering over Otavalo. This inactive volcano is about 4,600 meters or 15,120 feet in elevation, often capped with snow when it peers through the clouds. The Imbabura volcano, locally revered as Taita Imbabura, is considered the sacred protector of the Otavaleños. The people in this region have a spiritual relationship with the land and with Taita Imbabura and Mama Cotacachi, a nearby volcano overlooking the town of Cotacachi. Together, these volcanoes represent the culture's male and female protectors.

We arrive at the bus terminal and taxi to Cardón Bajo, where the Mendoza family lives. Their home is marked by a low, fenced-in brick building. Barking dogs and running chickens wander the patio. When Napo shouts, "Hello!" a dozen family members emerge, all crying out with delight.

They are dressed in traditional Otavaleño garb. The women wear white embroidered blouses, black shawls, wide colorful cummerbunds, and long dark-blue skirts; each has her hair tied into a single braid. They also wear traditional *walkas*, layers of necklaces of predominantly gold beads. The men dress in loose dark pants and white shirts, ponchos, and dark felt fedora hats. They tie their hair into *shimbas*, long braids that hang down to their waists, a symbol of Indigenous ethnic identity. Despite the cool climate, they wear *alpargatas*, shoes made from penko cactus fiber with black cloth tops and woven soles.

Their huge smiles and hugs immediately make me feel welcome. They take us into their humble house, where a bedroom also serves as a living room. The small children playfully climb over us when we sit on the bed.

Family members come and go, all wanting a glimpse of the new American stranger. Once again, I am thankful I can speak Spanish and easily chat with my hosts, answering their many questions.

The house is made of brick, a concrete slab, exposed walls, and dirt floors. Tattered prints are taped to the wall, and unraveling textiles cover holes. By any measure, the family is poor, but that doesn't seem to matter. The family numbers about forty members, although not all of them live here. An outdoor patio echoes with the sounds of chickens and roosters scattered everywhere, and there is scuffling and squeaking from makeshift cages containing about twenty guinea pigs. A boxlike structure with a tin roof serves as the bathroom.

The family serves lunch on a card table they pull into the bedroom. Carlos and Napo are served guinea pig—a local delicacy—and roasted potatoes. I have to look away, wondering about the cages I saw outside. I am grateful when Megan and I are served one of my favorite soups, *caldo de gallina criolla*, or hen soup, a delicious light broth with chicken, yucca, vegetables, and herbs.

Maria, the young woman whose daughter will later become my goddaughter, fiddles with her apron strings as she watches us eat. "*Todo bien?*" she asks with her head bowed.

"*Delicioso. Dios te bendiga*," I respond with the traditional thank-you.

Maria is twenty-five years old and a mother of two. She and her sister Lucia live here with their families. They are strong but humble women who manage to work and care for everyone else. A deep respect rises within me, recognition of the responsibilities that women worldwide take on for their families and communities. I am touched by the reverence with which they serve us the meal. In time, I will grow to understand that food is sacred when gifted to another in this manner. Cooked into the meal is all the effort of raising the animal, the time devoted to caring for the garden, and the affection the cook sprinkles into the dish. Sharing this meal is about more than eating; it's a sign of appreciation and acceptance.

After our meal, we distribute clothing from the large bag we brought with us. I have contributed clothes that I know I will not miss or need. The family's laughter and smiles fill the room. It feels like Christmas, and we visitors are Santa Claus. Before today, I didn't know how fulfilling it is to bring such joy to others. I leave with the gifts of grace and gratitude to the family.

We promise to return another day and leave with both our hearts and our bellies full. We catch a taxi to Peguche, a large park known for its walking trails, and the Cascada de Peguche, the waterfall where Inti Raymi purification ceremonies occur in June, on the solstice. This area is also steeped in ritual and spirituality for the local people. Their spiritual beliefs are connected to the earth's life force. The elements of land and water represent the aspects of vitality that flow to the people.

We enter the park and follow the paved trail toward the waterfall. As Napo and I discuss my impressions of the family, Carlos and Megan walk ahead. We are soon separated from them and continue toward the waterfall. Napo shares stories about the purification ceremonies that were held there and explains how the shamans would come together during the solstice in ancient times when there were no crowds or commercialism.

For a time, we walk silently, holding hands. It feels like we are walking both alone and together, an opening to something familiar but also new, full of potential and danger. I have never felt this way before. I caution myself not to dive into this relationship, only to discover it is a kind of rebound or a relief to the pain and emptiness I have felt since my divorce. I know we are connected by a deep spirituality I have never been able to articulate or define. It feels like the truth, as if it is the only real thing in my life.

As we turn into a curve on the path, I say, "Napo, tell me about shamanism. What is it, really? I want to understand. And I want to understand you."

Napo pauses momentarily and then motions for us to sit on a bench tucked into the bushes.

"Shamanism is simply to be present in life," he explains. "It's an integrated life, aligned within the principle of *unidad/totalidad* (singularity/wholeness). The divinity of the Creator is in us, and we are held in the divinity of the Creator. We are all children of the Creator. We have divine genes."

He pauses for a moment and turns to me. His eyes look at me as if he has discovered every secret I've ever held hidden in the space of my consciousness.

"You will try to interpret this based on the intellect and what you know; if you do that, you will never understand. Shamanism is based on *sentimiento*, feelings, and sensing that we and every living thing are children of the Creator. Our lives are the expression of that universal love. If you understand this, you will see your life as a path toward returning home. You will see yourself as a spiritual warrior. Your spiritual process is to commune with that divinity and to establish your existence as a conscious being, a representation of the Creator."

As I listen, I imagine my life's trajectory like a movie. He is speaking directly about my quest to recover the soul I thought I had lost when my spirit became matter, the transition from the universal womb into the human womb.

He continues, "At the shamanic level, consciousness has a practical reason. Consciousness is the memory of the Spirit. It's the initial memory, the gene of the Creator. Someone who is not spiritual is like someone with dementia. They cannot remember who or where they are, or why they are here. Your American culture has spiritual Alzheimer's."

His words feel like a blow, although I'm uncertain if he means it that way. His tone is pragmatic. But looking into his eyes, I notice a flash of anger followed by a deep breath and a shift to sadness. He rises from the bench, and we continue our walk.

Turning to me a few steps later, he says, "If you have no memory of the God origin, you have no connection with spirit. I must stay connected to my initial spiritual memory to help others recover theirs. I must access my inner spiritual warrior in the unconscious and the shadows. I go there to heal myself. This causes suffering because the mind and body resist. Consciousness is superior to mind and body and punishes them."

The intensity of his words unsettles me. I am grateful to walk again. I look away at times, feeling as if the natural surroundings might comfort me or reveal the deeper meaning behind his words without producing discomfort at what feels like a warning.

He continues, "That is why when a shaman is in the world, he must integrate and record the memories of the diversity of humanity. We are observers and witnesses. Shamans see how the microbial process, what you call evolution, is happening, and we record the process like a scientist. The shaman uses this knowledge as medicine for the world. We are the interpreters, the teachers, and the doctors of the soul."

We stop at another bench by the side of the path. I sit attentively and quietly, trying to hush my mind and feel his words. Based on my experiences as a child in my Colombian family, I intuitively understand what he means. Yet I have difficulty grasping how my world and his world could collaborate or collide.

My curiosity is piqued. "How did you know you were a shaman?"

He breathes deeply, and his body shifts like an animal poised to defend itself. "I had several episodes that awakened me at different times," he replies. "In my early twenties, I had an extraordinary experience where my consciousness merged with the universal consciousness. Imagine a million orgasms. It was like a cosmic orgasm, an infinite ecstasy. It was not the momentary pleasure of a human orgasm. It was a permanent memory, *gozo*, because consciousness knows that memory is of a divine origin through love. It took me over twenty years to wake up, to get over that experience, and enter my humanness again."

I can't imagine having that kind of experience. In a way, I envy it, accessing this universal oneness and feeling the ecstasy of merging the material and spiritual. But, at the same time, it scares the hell out of me.

"How do you return from that and live in this world?" I ask.

He peers toward the woods. His eyes fill with sadness, looking away as if seeing something I cannot see. His energy becomes still, and he answers succinctly. "I suffer."

At that moment, a voice calls from down the path. It's Carlos urging us to leave. Noticing a tear escaping Napo's eye, I take his hand and say nothing, speaking in the language of silence that first connected us. We continue down the path, calling to our friends that we are on our way.

The following day, I wake up feeling tired and a bit sick. Megan knocks sharply at my hotel door, calling, "Hurry up and get dressed. We're joining our Otavalo family for a traditional Ecuadorian cookout at Lago San Pablo. They'll be here soon with transportation. Dress warm!"

I feel sluggish. "Do I have to go? I'm not feeling well, and I'd like to sit this one out."

"Yes, you have to go," she replies sternly. "This is a big deal for Napo and Carlos. Get dressed."

I drag myself into the shower, and the hot water revives me. I pull on my warm leggings, a shirt, a warm sweatshirt, and sneakers and grab my daypack. I am ready in thirty minutes.

I stop at the hotel restaurant for breakfast and, most importantly, a cup of strong coffee. A blast of Ecuador's finest blend wakes me. Everyone is in the hotel lobby when I arrive.

There is so much excitement. About twenty family members—adults, children, and grandparents—are chattering away. As I approach, all eyes turn to me. Napo leads me to the group and introduces me to everyone. Many of them are extended family that I had not met the day before.

A small, thin older woman dressed in black pushes her way through the group. Flashing a toothless smile, her wrinkly eyes shining and blanketed arms reaching out, she hugs me. For such a tiny woman, the grandmother is strong. Her rapid-fire words come at me as her embrace grows tighter, and she shakes me back and forth, smiling and laughing. I hadn't expected such a playful greeting, and her joy dispels my earlier funk. It isn't until this moment, with this grandmother's blessing, that I realize they believe I am Napo's *novia*, girlfriend.

We depart the hotel and walk to the large truck parked down the street. The canvas that covers the rear of the vehicle is pulled back, revealing an empty cargo space. "This is our transportation?" I ask nervously.

"Yes," replies Carlos. "But don't worry. You and Megan can ride in the front seat as our guests."

Once the family is loaded into the back, a cacophony of voices and laughter seep into the front seat as the truck lurches forward. Megan and I exchange glances of amusement, unable to stifle our giggles. Later, Napo explains that they had been teasing him, indicating that I have been accepted.

Our first stop is Mojanda, an inactive volcano in the eastern cordillera of the Andes, occupied by three crater lakes: Karikucha, Yanakucha, and Warmikucha. These are sacred sites for the Otavalo people, each with its own mythology. The lake waters are as smooth as a mirror, reflecting the clouds above. Napo informs me that the waters are icy, especially this time of year. He recalls, "When we were young and would visit, we would dive into the cold waters simply to feel the aliveness of the lake and drink from the energy of the volcano." We are in the *páramo*, the grasslands above the cloud forests. I am surprised at how cold it is. I see my breath float from my mouth like wispy vapers.

Just beyond our parking spot, I notice small food stands under a canopy made from scraps of material. Steam rising from their make-shift stoves and the fragrant smell of something unknown floats in the air, making my stomach growl.

"How would you like to try *choclo*, Alicia?" Napo asks with a broad smile. "It will warm you up." *Choclo* is roasted corn with kernels that are larger, chewier, and starchier than sweet corn. The woman behind the stove serves the corn in small plastic cups, the kind you usually drink from, and sprinkles it with spices I have never tasted before. Napo brings me *morocho*, a traditional hot, thick, sweet drink made with cracked corn, milk, cinnamon, sugar, and raisins. The heat and spice of the *choclo* and *morocho* are just what I need to appease my growing hunger and keep away the chill of the mountain air.

After a short stroll to the water's edge and back, we are ready to drive to Lago San Pablo, a mythical lake surrounded by the majesty of the mountains. The group sings and laughs as they climb into the back of the truck. Within thirty minutes, we arrive at the lake's picnic area. The women begin to unload cooking utensils, pots, pans, and plates while the men unload small grills and large bags of food.

An open-air shelter awaits us, and the cooking and feasting begin. I watch as the women stoke fires beneath grill plates that have been placed over piles of rocks. The flames rise as they cook skewers of meat and plantains and, in large pots, cook potatoes, yucca, and rice. I am in awe of what is unfolding. As if choreographed, they work in tandem, each knowing their contribution to the process. The women joke, gossip, and giggle as they cook. I imagine these resilient women would help their families survive any disaster. The longer I spend in Ecuador, the more I appreciate the Indigenous women's strength, loy-alty, and love for their families and communities.

Napo taps me on the shoulder, inviting me to walk with him into a nearby field. He motions for us to sit on the ground. "I hope you are enjoying our trip. Wait until you taste the food," he exclaims, practi-cally salivating. Four of the children approach, and one who is about

ten years old, Pamelita, embraces Napo and refuses to release him. She
sits between us, silently protesting my closeness to him. Napo shares
that he is especially close to her. She almost died when she was four,
and the family credits the shamans with saving her.

I speak to the children in Spanish, and they chirp like little chicks.
One boy, about four, with rose-colored cheeks that look like little bal-
loons, grabs my hand and pulls me toward the lake. I humor him as he
chats wildly and incoherently. His happiness infuses me with the same
childlike wonder as he digs in the dirt near the water.

I offer him the hotel crackers I had stuffed into my pockets. "*Más*,"
he repeats, indicating that he wants more. We run back to Napo,
where Pamelita and Diana, her cousin, watch a few young boys playing soccer. I distribute the crackers. You would have thought I was
giving out gold. The little boy with rosy cheeks tiptoes around me and,
grinning, puts a yellow flower over my ear. My heart breaks as wide
open as the landscape, the children's happiness reflected in their eyes
like the reflection of clouds in the lake. I am bathed in the lightness of
simply being with family, even if they aren't mine.

The women summon us to eat, distributing the food on plastic dishes.
No utensils, only small napkins, accompany the plates loaded with
food. The men are served first, and their meals are heavy with meat,
while the women wait until the end and eat what is left. In a gesture
that speaks louder than words, Napo hands me his plate and waits for
the next dish to be served. The women eye him, then me, and give him
another plate overflowing with chunks of meat. They smile knowingly
as he receives it, saying, "*Dios te bendiga.*"

The afternoon is filled with food, chatter, play, music, and dancing.
Then the women gather the cooking items. No food is left. I approach
the woman who led the cooking and thank her, extending my hand
when she stands up. She holds my hand in hers and then hugs me. A
silent approval floats beyond her deep, dark eyes.

The air cools and the light of day slowly fades. Everything is loaded into the truck for the trip back to Otavalo. Again, as the guest of honor, I ride in the front seat. Driving along roads where the last glimmers of light seep between the eucalyptus trees lulls me into a gentle preamble to the evening. I hear faint chatter from the rear compartment until it, too, fades into quiet.

It takes forty-five minutes to return to our hotel in Otavalo. I'm happy but tired, feeling my heart nourished by the food, company, and nature. Napo escorts me to my room, where we talk about the day for a few minutes.

"Today reminded me of when I was ten in Colombia with my mother," I tell him. "Her family would take us on these kinds of outings. I always left feeling happy, cared for, and loved. I feel like that today too."

"You'll sleep well tonight, and we'll return to Quito tomorrow. I'm glad you enjoyed my adopted family. I'm sure you will be seeing them again."

I unlock the door and pause, sensing that he might say something else. We are in the hall, feeling connected despite the space between us. We stand this way for about a minute. Then he says, "I will wait to make sure your door is locked. We'll have breakfast at eight tomorrow morning."

"Thank you for a lovely day, Napo, one I will always remember." I quietly close the door and listen as he jiggles the doorknob from the other side, testing the lock. I hear his footsteps as he walks to his room a few doors down the hall. Then, with a click, his door opens and closes. As I listen, I can't help but wonder about the doors in my life that are just beginning to open and close.

– 5 –
WHAT THE PYRAMIDS BLESSED

If you could trust your soul, you would receive every blessing you require. Life itself is the great sacrament through which we are wounded and healed.

—John O'Donohue

You don't negotiate with destiny.

Your path will emerge, surprising your best-laid plans. You'll live for years with the illusion of control over your life. You'll believe in your dreams and be meticulous about your decisions, assuring you reach your goals.

That is, until they're hijacked by the simplest decision, made on a whim, with no apparent significance. Then, suddenly, you'll find yourself groundless, uncertain about everything, and if you allow fear to overtake you, you'll lose out on the unexpected experience that life has gifted you.

My time in Ecuador was that turning point, the crossroads I didn't recognize. The choice to go there, which I made on a whim, caused an upheaval in my life that I never could have foreseen. And yet I chose to take the alternative path despite my fear of the unknown, avoiding friends' well-intentioned comments and rejecting my attachments to the way I felt my life should be.

The clues to a different kind of life had been there all along. Like threads in a tapestry woven by an omniscient weaver, each experience, each dream, was creating my life—bringing me to Ecuador, a country I had never considered visiting, and to a shaman who would heal me with his light and wound me with his shadow.

In one prescient dream that recurred while I was in my forties, years before my trip to Ecuador, I was hiking a mountain. The landscape was a deep and vibrant green. There was an occasional boulder and rocks that caused me to veer in many directions, but I always moved up. Through the clouds, I glimpsed the top of the mountain, which was covered in snow. I was always cold—the kind of cold that feels like glass in your lungs and makes it difficult to breathe.

I fell and couldn't get up. I was on my knees when I heard someone approach. Climbing toward me with a determined pace, holding a staff with a tiger's head carved at the top, was a man dressed in a bright-red wool poncho adorned with beading and colored ribbons. He wore an old black fedora-style hat, battered and dirty, like a crown. He announced his presence with each step, a demand to be acknowledged by the mountain. His pants barely covered his sandals, and I couldn't help but wonder if his feet were cold.

When he reached me, he looked down with disdain and said something in a language I intuited but couldn't understand. It felt like a physical push or jab. He was brusque with me, challenging me to get up. His voice was as sharp as the cliff's cutting edges. I extended my hand, a request for assistance, but he batted it away with the staff. He turned, leaving me with my hand floating in the air, my heart crushed.

Even then, I knew he was a shaman. I couldn't predict that I would meet this man in my fifties and spend eight years with him. I didn't know he would teach me to rise and finally save myself.

Ecuador is a land steeped in spirituality. Before the Spanish arrived with their Catholicism, the shamans were their tribes' spiritual leaders.

Today, forty-two diverse tribes, each with its own culture, dress, gastronomy, and spiritual traditions, comprise the country's Indigenous population. Sacred sites can be found throughout Ecuador, ranging from archaeological digs on the coast to large structures hidden in the rainforests.

One of the oldest and most well-known archaeological sites is Cochasquí, a complex of fifteen pyramids and twenty-one burial mounds called *tolas*, located twenty miles northeast of Quito. Archaeologists believe the Quitu-Cara people built Cochasquí as a ceremonial and astronomical center used to calculate solstices and determine the planting and harvesting seasons. But little beyond that is known.

The Luna brothers descended from the Quitu-Cara people. For generations, the Luna family conducted ceremonies at Cochasquí during the equinoxes and solstices, attracting thousands from around the world. They convened meetings between South American shamans to discuss politics and perform rituals to heal the planet. They were the wisdom keepers of Cochasquí, the knowers of the secrets hidden in the pyramids and the sacred geometry of the structures. For them, this land was holy, an energetic and magnetic portal into the transcendent worlds where they would travel during these ceremonies.

Toward the end of my stay, Napo invites me to Cochasquí. That morning, as I get ready in the bathroom, I overhear Carlos and Napo in the kitchen, arguing. The walls are thin enough that I can hear their conversation.

"No, this isn't right," Carlos says vehemently. "You don't really know her. You've only just met her. You should not do this!"

"Brother, I want you by my side," Napo answers. "This encounter with Alicia was destined. She and I have always been connected in time and space. We have met in dreams and past lives. I want to formalize our bond so no matter where we are, we remain together."

"You're infatuated, brother. It is blinding you. I cannot agree with this. I will go, but I will not participate. This is not right. I have not been happy with the way both of you are behaving. This is not right." Clearly, Carlos isn't pleased with how my relationship with Napo has grown.

I leave the bathroom unnoticed and go upstairs to my room to dress. I'm worried. What does Napo want to do, and why does it cause Carlos such concern?

When I come downstairs, Megan is sitting outside in the sunshine. She looks up at me with displeasure. "Aren't you coming?" I ask her.

"I don't want to go, and I don't want you to go either," she answers.

"I'm confused," I reply. "Have I done something wrong?"

Megan stands as she scolds me. "I invited you here to translate for Napo so he could help me with my dissertation. I never expected you would begin a romance with him."

"Wait a minute," I say firmly. "I've been asking when we would do the work, and you haven't answered me. I didn't start this thing with Napo. I've done no harm. We have a mutual connection, and I believe it's based on care. Our conversations are about deep things—shamanism, spirituality, and meaning-of-life things. I am always respectful. I don't understand why you and Carlos are angry with me."

From indoors, Carlos calls to her. Megan turns away from me. As she enters the apartment, she passes Napo, who exits holding a leather pouch, a blanket, and a glass bottle containing a dark liquid with sprigs of herbs.

"What's going on, Napo?" I ask. "I'm confused. Have I done something wrong?"

"No, you haven't done anything wrong. Carlos is simply being protective of me."

"Protecting you against what? Against me?" I'm torn between being angry that I'm being blamed for something unknown and being sad that Carlos, whom I care for as a brother, and Megan, whom I've known for many years, are treating me like I've done something terrible. It reminds me of my teenage years when my parents disapproved of the boys I brought home. But here I am, a mature single woman who feels like I've been discovered sneaking back home in the early morning hours after a surreptitious night out.

Napo explains why Carlos and Megan are acting strangely. "Shamans must be very careful with the people around them. Our energies will intermingle, harming the shaman and the other person if the intention is not honorable. I intend to conduct a ceremony at Cochasquí that formalizes the connection we know existed in another time and place. Cochasquí is the land of my ancestors, a sacred place we have guarded for generations. It is my spiritual home on earth. Here, I invite you to share my life in the presence of my ancestors and the spirits that guide me."

I've begun to care deeply for Napo in a way I've never felt before. I'm sure he's the guide I had searched for, someone who can help me resolve this schism between the sacred and secular that kept me searching for the divine. Our relationship seems to be moving fast, maybe too fast. Yet I can't deny that it feels like the only true thing in my life.

My conversations with Napo give me a new way of understanding my childhood experiences, which always felt natural to me at the time even though most people would have considered them out of the ordinary. I can't shake the feeling that somewhere I've lost my way. Long ago, I gave up looking for gurus, teachers, or guides, always disappointed with the commercialism of spirituality and the phoniness of the New Age movement. Without any intention or plan, I've met Napo, the shaman who appeared in my dreams years ago and is now inviting me into the deeper connection I long for.

Suddenly, with Megan and Carlos's reprimand, I feel that what I've gained in Ecuador is being taken away. Guilt rises into my throat, choking any words I might speak to defend myself. I'd begun the day feeling hopeful, but now my body buckles from the possibility of losing the understanding that feels so close at hand.

As the four of us pile into the taxi that morning, no one says anything about my conversation with Megan, or Megan's declaration that she wasn't coming, or the disagreement between Napo and Carlos. Napo carries the pouch containing the blanket and bottle. Carlos sits in the front seat, chatting with the driver, as the rest of us sit in the back. It takes almost an hour to arrive at Cochasquí.

At the gate, we are met by the complex's guardian, José. He is a short, slight man with a weathered face, furry mustache, and gray hair covered by a baseball cap. He is dressed warmly, in layers, and a long lanyard around his neck holds a collection of keys. Recognizing the brothers, he opens the taxi door and hugs each man affectionately. "*Hola, hombre.* It's been a long time since I've seen you," he says to Carlos. Then, turning to Napo, giving him a long hug and placing a firm hand on his back, he says, "And where have you been, my friend? You have been missed."

"We are here to show our women the land and teach them about our ancestors," Carlos tells José.

"You have the best guides," José says to Megan and me, smiling and clapping his hands.

Once through the gate, we approach a bamboo, wood, and stone structure. The museum houses a collection of artifacts and models. Pottery, textiles, and stone tools are displayed in glass boxes and cement tables. A table about six feet long by four feet across holds a three-dimensional model of the complex, the pyramids, and the other structures.

José explains that the primary construction material used in the pyramids is a soft volcanic stone called *cangahua*. Vulnerable to weathering and erosion, the pyramids survive because they are overgrown with grass and moss. The entrances are sealed to keep thieves from stealing the artifacts. He points to the model's largest pyramid, number nine. This pyramid measures 300 feet north to south, 260 feet east to west, and 69 feet high. The ramp leading to the pyramid is 660 feet long. Even in the model, it seems like an imposing structure. José claims this pyramid is the most significant in the complex but doesn't explain why.

After a history lesson from José, where he recounts the stories of the Quitu-Cara tribes and the site's significance, we leave to walk the land. As we enter the main complex, a panorama of hills appears in front of us. Hundreds of llamas, black, brown, and white, graze over the expanse of the complex. The land is covered in brush, and yellow-green grass covers the mounds. Cochasquí is 9,970 feet above sea level, and with an unobstructed view, we can see Quito in front of us. Beyond Quito, the Andes protrude from the city haze below to stand under the downy clouds covering the sky.

It's cold and windy, and it begins to drizzle. Undeterred, we start our walk with Napo explaining the significance of the complex and his ancestry. Carlos and Megan quietly separate from us despite moving in the same direction. Napo looks briefly toward them, then returns to his storytelling.

"We come from the Quitu-Cara tribe, a tribe of warriors and wisdom keepers. Our lineage is through our mother. In our culture, the land was passed down through the women, and the women governed. The Quitu-Cara tribe disappeared with the arrival of the Spanish in the 1500s. We refused to give the Incas or Spanish the secrets of the Shyris, the people of light from which we are descendants. We have kept the secrets of Cochasquí hidden."

As we walk, I feel the energy of the place surrounding me. Hidden in Napo's words and the sounds of nature is silence as old as these pyramids. I imagine what ceremonies may have occurred here in ancient times, the songs for the harvests, and the blessings that connected the people to the Pachamama, as the earth is known in Ecuador.

I walk this ancient place with a man I met only a few days ago. This man has touched my heart and discovered my soul in hiding, reverently holding a space for love to appear.

I am near tears listening to Napo's stories when we stop and he says, simply, "Here."

We are at the top of the seventh pyramid on a flat space of earth facing out toward the Andes. I watch Megan and Carlos step toward the edge of the area, turning their backs as they sit, looking toward the horizon. I realize this is what Carlos meant in the kitchen when he argued with Napo. They choose not to participate in or approve of the ceremony.

Napo spreads the blanket on the ground with each corner facing one of the cardinal directions, north, south, east, and west. He reaches into his leather pouch and carefully removes several items. He places seashells, pieces of wood, miniature animal carvings, symbols etched on stones, flowers, rattles, and an ocarina on the blanket. Then he pulls a colorful headband from the pouch and wraps it around his head, protecting his shoulder-length hair from the wind. In a stone bowl, he places sticks of palo santo, a sweet-smelling wood burned to sanctify an area and clean its energy. He lights the palo santo and fans it with a large feather so that the smoke rises as he walks around the blanket chanting. The wind plays with the smoke as if greeting an old friend with a hug that spins the friend around and around.

"Come and kneel here," Napo commands as he motions for me to come to the middle of the blanket. He blows the palo santo around himself and me, then sets the bowl down and kneels to face me.

"Alicia, we are connected and have always been connected. I've seen our past lives and now understand why I felt the surge of energy when you hugged me at the airport when you arrived. I invite you to bond with me through this ceremony to formalize the connection between our souls so I can forever protect, teach, and heal you. From me, you will learn the true meaning of love, not human love, but *el sentimiento universal*, the love that is passed to us from the Creator."

Tears stream down my face. I feel lightheaded, drunk on the energy that rises from the ground as I kneel on this sacred land. The shaman has appeared. It is as if Napo has transcended physical space and emerged as an ancient form. I lose all time, all sense of physical space. Not entirely in my body, I see and hear him from somewhere else.

"Do you accept my invitation?"

His question echoes through my trance, and I hear my voice say, "Yes."

Napo stands and begins to chant in Quechua, the Indigenous language of his people. He chants and dances with the rattles while the wind blows clouds of palo santo and sprays raindrops, enveloping us in an otherworldly mist. He opens the bottle containing the dark liquid and herbs and, without swallowing it, takes it into his mouth. Then he sprays me and the area around us with this liquid that smells of cinnamon and roses. He raises the ocarina to his lips and plays a tune unlike anything I have ever heard, the notes vibrating in the wind, raindrops dancing to the music.

I don't know how long the ceremony lasts. It seems as if this moment on top of a sacred pyramid in the middle of the world is all that exists, a blessing witnessed by the ancestors and ancient wisdom keepers. As tears slide down my face, Napo kneels next to me, hugs me, and, taking my face in his hands, whispers into my ear, "*El amor vence todo.*" Love will always prevail.

His words jolt me out of the trance. Around my neck, I wear a small locket I have carried for seventeen years, bought when my son was born. Tucked inside the locket is a small piece of paper inscribed with a prayer I wrote. It's only three words: "May love prevail."

The cup of tea feels pleasant in my hands. I am still recovering from the chill of being at Cochasquí in the rain. Steam rises from the cup, and a fragrant scent of chamomile tickles my nose. Wrapped in a warm blanket on the small sofa in the front room of Carlos's apartment, Napo and I speak quietly about the ceremony at the pyramids.

Carlos and Megan are cleaning up in the kitchen after a light dinner of soup and bread. The tension from the ride back had continued through the meal. Carlos only mentions the day's events once. "It was too soon. We won't speak of it again." With that, the subject is closed.

The soothing effect of chamomile tea begins to take effect. Then, noticing my yawn, Napo says good night to his brother and leads me, still wrapped in the blanket, up the stairs to my room.

"You will have dreams tonight, Alicia," he declares. "If you remember them, we can talk about them tomorrow." We stand in the doorway, and he gives me a light kiss on the cheek. "*Buenas noches*," he says tenderly, closing the door, and leaves.

I don't change out of my clothes. The room is still, and cold penetrates my body, removing all traces of warmth from the tea. Getting into bed, I pull the blankets over my head. Darkness draws me into a long tunnel, and I tumble into unconsciousness until the sun revives me the following morning. I do not remember any dreams. All I recall are the echoes of the wind on the top of the sacred pyramid.

– 6 –
PANTERITA

It feels like a clock has stopped. Dreams mix with memories in a blur of still photographs behind my eyes. My face is buried in my pillow, a rebellious act against the beams of sunlight flooding my room. I don't want to get up. I don't want to move. I don't want to leave Ecuador.

Tap. Tap. Tap. "*Hola*, Alicia, *levántese!*" It's Napo outside my door, humor in his voice as he calls to me. He announces breakfast with one more bang on the door.

"Okay, *ya voy!*" I call from under the sheets, hoping my response will cause him to go downstairs. I wipe the sleep from my eyes and crawl into yesterday's sweatshirt and pants, which are recklessly lying on the chair. A few minutes later, I gingerly navigate the stairs, which are slippery from the moisture that accumulated during last night's shower. The house smells strongly of coffee and fresh bread. I suddenly notice the emptiness in my stomach begging to be filled.

Everyone is at the table, already eating. "*Hola, buenos días,*" I say. My words are as slow as my pace. Between bites, they respond with "*Buenas,*" using a shortened version of the greeting to minimize interruptions to their eating.

I have only one day left in Ecuador. I look over at Napo, already missing him. This surprises me. Between bites and some commentary lies doubt, nostalgia, and confusion. *Now what?* I wonder. After I leave, then what?

Carlos interrupts my reverie. "Today, we're going to have an easy day. We'll visit Parque La Carolina, have lunch in Quito, and walk around. The sun will come out soon. Bring a hat. It will get warmer in a few hours, and the sun will feel very strong." With our agenda set, we venture out an hour later, grabbing a yellow taxi to the Carapungo neighborhood, where we pick up the bus to the center of Quito.

I wear my backpack in front, over my chest and stomach, to keep my belongings safe. Crowded buses are a pickpocket's playground. I smile, noticing that my balance has improved as the bus sways violently from side to side. *I'm getting the hang of this*, I think. *Just in time to leave*, chides my mind.

The center of Quito is bustling, and I wonder why people think of Ecuador as a third-world country. High in the Andes, this city is full of commerce and energy. I notice the office workers, women with long jet-black hair in tight dresses and impossibly high heels, and men dressed in hipster clothes or Wall Street suits. Quito looks like most cities, with nothing third-world about it.

We enter La Carolina, the largest park in Quito, which is full of people at midday. I notice the contrast between humble Ecuadorian families out for a leisurely picnic and the obvious foreigners jogging in their Adidas sneakers and high-end Nike running suits. It's Friday, and the weekend has already begun. Carts full of fast food, empanadas, *pinchos*, and fruit-filled cups line the park. Their owners are shouting, "Come, I have empanadas! The best juices! Come, let me offer you something!" They remind me of carnival hawkers with their colorful clothes and boisterous pitches.

La Carolina is a lush, green 165-acre oasis in the center of the steel and concrete buildings of the city's business district. This is where Quiteños gather, mostly during the weekends, for outdoor activities and exercise. With its various sporting areas, art installations, and playgrounds, there's something here for everyone. The southern end is home to a pond where romantic couples paddleboat and a ubiquitous skateboard park where all the dudes in baggy pants, Vans sneakers, and backward baseball caps hang out. For the more erudite, there are diverse trees, many with signs indicating their Latin names and genus to provide lessons in dendrology. The botanical garden, *jardín botánico*, is a hidden jewel, a masterpiece of flora and fauna featuring rose displays, exotic orchids, carnivorous plants, and a stunning Japanese bonsai garden.

Loud shouting catches our attention. On a large field, young men—and not-so-young men—are playing *fútbol*. Both Carlos and Napo had been soccer players earlier in life. Carlos reached national prominence in the 1970s as one of the country's most feared players. He was built like a tank, belying the velocity at which he could run. His opponents nicknamed him El Perro, "The Dog," for his refusal to give up the ball to anyone. Napo chose to support his younger brother as his coach instead of becoming a professional player himself. They're still soccer fanatics with extreme opinions about how the game should be played.

We stop to watch for a while, with the brothers narrating a running commentary between shouting insults at players. Perfectly normal in Ecuador.

Hunger is never far away, so after a half hour of shouting, we find somewhere to eat. Getting away from the main streets and franchised restaurants, we find *una hueca*, a hole-in-the-wall. Here, we can find the cheapest and most authentic food. We sit at a table covered with a plastic floral tablecloth, the kind used at outdoor barbeques, and place our order. The women cook in the back while their grown children serve hungry clients in the restaurant. An order of *almuerzo*, the plate of the day, runs about three dollars and is the go-to order for a meal hot from the stove. It doesn't disappoint. Our first course is a deep bowl of soup, a broth with a hunk of meat and potatoes. After that, the server brings the brothers more meat over a mound of rice, a soft plantain called *maduro*, and a tall glass of freshly squeezed lemonade. Megan and I choose braised chicken breast over rice with plantains as our main course. A lemon flan and a cup of coffee complete the meal. Feeling full, we walk off our lunch by browsing a few shops. Napo suggests we find a place for a drink, and we head to La Mariscal, Quito's nightlife district, full of bars and restaurants.

For a moment, my life at home comes into view. Right now, I might be getting ready for drinks and dinner with my girlfriends. We'd be walking down Main Street as the sun set, heading to a favorite restaurant. We'd share our triumphs and look to each other for advice on our newest client or relationship over an appetizer of burrata and a rich Malbec. I smile as I consider the irony of being a thousand miles and a lifetime away, wondering which life I belong to.

Loud music points us to La Foch, a plaza at the center of the entertainment district. The competition for the best sound system drowns out even the traffic noise. We find a bar appropriately named El Gringo and settle into a small table for four to order drinks and listen to the music. Soon we're taking shots of tequila between beers. I remind myself that I must leave for the airport at five in the morning, and naturally, I have not yet packed my bags.

After a few hours, Carlos announces in an authoritative voice that it's time to go home. "Remember, Alicia has to leave at five in the morning." Then, turning to me, he says seriously, "You need your sleep." His look indicates that our departure is nonnegotiable. Pooling together what is left of our money, we take a taxi home.

We return tired but happy. I feel high and woozy, having celebrated my last night in Ecuador. Carlos and Megan retreat to their living space with a simple good night. "I'll walk up with you," Napo tells me, motioning toward the stairs. As I open the door to my room, he places his hand on my shoulder and says, "Can I come in? I'd like to talk to you."

I pause. There are competing voices screaming in my head: "No, thank you. It was a wonderful evening, and I have to get up early. I'm sure we can talk tomorrow on the way to the airport." And "Sure. Come in for a while, and maybe I can pack while we talk."

The second one speaks out loud. I let him in.

My eyes take a moment to adjust to the room's darkness. I stumble to the small table with the needlepoint doily and the antique lamp and turn it on. Shadows bounce off the painted concrete walls. A knot forms in my stomach, and I begin to tremble.

"Are you cold?" he asks through the immense stillness that seems to surround him. It's a sharp contrast to my vision. Everything seems to be moving and looks blurry and distorted, as if I am underwater. "Maybe you should sit down," he suggests, gently leading me to the bed.

The back of my neck tingles, and my mind struggles to penetrate the fog. Napo brings me an open bottle of water that has been sitting on a shelf all day. The temperature in the room has kept it cool, and the chilled liquid seems to calm the fire in my body. I drink the entire bottle as he sits beside me, relaxed, observing, and still.

"Tomorrow morning, you will leave Ecuador and return to your life. What will you take with you?"

I gaze into the deep pool of darkness behind his eyes, curious to know if this is a test. Slowly, I stand and remove my jacket as my body begins to generate intense heat from my solar plexus. I fumble for an answer. I want to sound wise, but I feel like a child, scared and confused.

The clock in the room ticks away the seconds, persistent, growing louder with each tick. It's as if time is tapping on my shoulder: *tap, tap, wake up, wake up*. A soft glow surrounds him even though the lamp is on the other side of the room. I'm in a trance now. I know it. It's not the wooziness and disconnection I feel when I've had too much to drink. I'm totally present.

He slowly leans forward, and I lose myself in the depths of his dark eyes. His hands cup my face, and his lips cover mine. Behind my closed eyes, I still see him. My lips respond softly at first, then with a hunger I thought had disappeared years ago. I'm falling deeper, deeper into my body, an unfamiliar place, deserted years ago in exchange for safety and peace. Every cell in my body comes alive, vibrating fiercely as we toss our clothes onto the floor. I'm overcome by the intense energy surging between us, an ancient force resurrected. My mind finally surrenders, and we merge like a symphony reaching its crescendo in perfect rhythm and timing.

The ticking is louder now, filling the room and competing with the sounds of our lovemaking. Hour after hour passes until a final exhaustion descends and silence returns. In the soft light, I can see tiny beads of sweat on his face, his hair damp against his unlined forehead. My trembling is gone, replaced with the cool stillness of the deepest lake, reminding me of Mojanda, the lake in the Andes we visited with his adopted family from Otavalo.

"What will you take with you?" he whispers, nuzzling my ear.

"You," is my only answer.

I don't notice what time he leaves. I fall into a deep slumber, my dreams filled with rainforests, rivers, soaring condors, and sacred pyramids. The man with the walking staff, still wearing a red poncho and black felt fedora, stands on a mountain ledge looking down at me. The sun is behind him. I can't see his face. He bangs his staff on the ridge, calling to me.

"Alicia. Alicia. Wake up! We leave in twenty minutes!" It's Napo, banging on my door. I sit up straight in my bed. As if someone had thrown icy water in my face, I fully awaken.

"Oh, shit!" I call through the closed door. I fumble for my watch, which I finally find on the table near the bed, and it reads 5:30 a.m. I was supposed to have left half an hour ago. "I have to pack! Give me fifteen minutes."

"Alicia, open the door."

I pull a blanket around my naked body and open the door. His eyes are serious at first, but then a broad smile fills his face and mischief glints in his eye.

"How are you today?" he asks, our secret encounter standing between us.

My head is throbbing, but I say, "Fine. I'm good."

"Pack quickly. The taxi will be here any minute. We can get breakfast at the airport." I'm surprised at how alert he is compared to my disheveled and unsteady state of mind.

"What about Carlos and Megan? Are they ready to go?" I ask.

A shadow crosses his eyes. "No, Alicia. They are not coming. It's best not to wake them. I will take you to the airport." His tone confirms my suspicion that they have not forgiven me for whatever sins I've committed. But at that moment, I don't care.

I pack quickly, and within twenty minutes, we're on our way to the airport. Without my morning coffee, I'm still half asleep and a bit hungover from the night before. Napo rides in the front seat with the driver, chatting amiably.

The memory of the previous night comes rushing back, and my body responds. Sensations left over from our lovemaking reignite in the back seat. *What the hell?* my inner voice says, angry that I cannot control my feelings. *I'm leaving. This shouldn't be happening to me, not now.*

When we arrive at the terminal, the driver pulls over. I get out and take my luggage from the trunk. I frantically search my backpack for my wallet and pay the driver while Napo rolls my bags to the sidewalk. There's no line when we bring the luggage to the counter and check in. We search for coffee and breakfast before I cross through security into the gate area.

Once we sit down with our coffee, it hits me that I am leaving, and I have no idea if I will ever see Napo again. He reads my mind.

"Panterita, will you ever come back to Ecuador?"

"Panterita?" I ask. "Why did you call me that?"

"That is my name for you now. Panthers are sacred animals in my culture. They demand respect and symbolize ancient wisdom and spiritual strength."

Not fully understanding, I ask, "But why would you call me that?"

"Every animal has their unique traits. The panther is a feminine archetypal symbol. The panther is fiercely protective of those she loves. Her courage knows no limits. And most importantly, she sees in the dark, like you." His eyes focus on mine as if nothing else exists in the room.

Noticing my confusion, he continues, "I know your fierceness now. I know your capacity for love. You are unafraid to go into dark places to heal yourself or others. That is why they come to you. You show them what courage looks like within the darkness they are experiencing. Your capacity for love makes them feel safe because you are walking with them in the darkness and will protect them."

Despite the sounds of the busy airport, I can only hear his voice. The tone and cadence of his words hypnotize me.

"Last night was a shamanic healing for you. I released the stagnant energy that some call kundalini. It has kept you from being creative and daring, like the *panterita* I know you are. You are returning more whole. You are returning as a spiritual warrior. And the panther will be at your side, guiding you."

A waterfall of emotions rushes toward me like a tsunami I am unprepared to meet. I sob quietly as my body heaves with emotion. He sits still, and only after a few moments does he reach out and take my hand across the table. Once again, we exchange no words. Instead, we communicate in the silent language that first connected us when he held my hand on a dark staircase in Quito earlier in the week.

"I love you, Panterita, even if we never see each other again. But not the human love you have known. I love you from the universal, spiritual love that is granted by the Creator and held in the heart of every creature. When you connect to that within yourself, like you did last night, you can be a true reflection for others to experience this spiritual love. Unlike human love that changes with time, this love that we call *amor propio* is infinite. Our most difficult lesson is to learn to love from *amor propio*, the love that is timeless, limitless, and truly spiritual in its essence because it begins within you, not with the other."

Napo then stands up and gently pulls me to my feet so I'm close to him. Leaning in, he continues to speak quietly. "Napo loves Alicia from the Creator's universal heartbeat, which is greater than the whole universe. My responsibility is to lead you by the hand to where you truly belong. Thank you for discovering true love."

The loudspeaker intrudes, announcing that it is time for me to board my flight. I don't want to go. I want to stay forever holding the hand of this shaman who has entered my life, and my heart, in such a profound manner. Sensing my hesitation, he embraces me and murmurs near my ear, "Alicia, it's time for you to return to your life in America. I go with you."

We walk toward my gate hand in hand. I wipe the tears from my face with a napkin I find in my pocket. Our farewell embrace reminds me of our merging the night before. The heat rises, and energy floods my body once again. We remain in a timeless space until he releases me, turns my body toward the departure gate, and abruptly turns and walks away. Just before I reach the agent, I look back, searching for him, hoping I might catch one last glimpse of the man who has awakened me, but all that remains of him is the fire still burning inside me.

– 7 –
NO PLACE OF BELONGING

A week after leaving Ecuador, I wake up in my apartment on the Chesapeake Bay with the sun shining through the blinds, nudging me from a deep sleep that only light can reach. Instead of burying my face in the pillow, I now cherish how the sun rises on the horizon, a bright orange orb reflecting hope for a new day.

My golden retriever, Finn, is already at my bedroom door, watching tentatively for any movement that signals breakfast is imminent. We have a ritual. He waits until my room fills with light and then he whines softly, unsure if I will respond. Once I'm up, I let him run outside to pee, and he bolts back up the circular stairs knowing his bowl will be full when he returns. Our morning ritual is one of the few things in my life that is certain and constant.

My morning coffee is brewing, and once my breakfast is ready, I sit at the small kitchen table, looking out at the towering oak tree framing the bay. It never matters whether the weather is sunny, rainy, or snowy. What matters is that dawn arrives every day, heralding a new possibility for my life. Besides Finn, sunrise and sunset are the only things I count on.

In the weeks that follow my return from Ecuador, I swing from the excitement of the new love I'd discovered with Napo to a longing for that love. My desire to continue working with client organizations has faded. There is an acute, painful contrast between my experience of being in the natural world in Ecuador and my work with corporate clients who are primarily interested in career advancement and profitability. I feel as if I am living a life designed for someone else. Business interactions feel uninspired, and I become intolerant of the people around me who are motivated by money, status, and ego.

In Ecuador, I discovered there was more to my life than work and the external trappings of success. Once tasted, the sweetness of a life that could be is irresistible. I cannot reconcile my life in the States with my experience of a more profound spiritual calling, insistent and distracting. The memory of my conception once again surfaces as an existential inquiry. I question the meaning of my existence. *Why am I here?*

In 1955, my parents immigrated to the United States. They came searching for the American dream. Although they had dated in Colombia, they enjoyed more of a friendship than a romance. They arrived in New York together, intending to go their separate ways once they reached America. My father planned to stay in New York City with his friend Oscar Soto, and my mother would travel to Massachusetts with her sister, Delia, and Delia's husband, Carlo.

Delia and Carlo met my parents in New York. Upon hearing my father's plans, Carlo offered to find him a job at the company where he worked in Watertown, Massachusetts. Considering the promise of a job, my father agreed to travel back to Watertown with them. But there was a catch. There was only one apartment, and my mother and father would need to live together. Living together before marriage wasn't done in those days, but it was convenient for them. They agreed to the arrangement, although my mother and her sister were cautious about the proposal.

When I was fifteen, my mother told me what happened next. She had grown lonely in Watertown. They had arrived in November; the trees were bare, the cold was setting in, and the days were short and dark. My mother would cry, thinking she'd made a mistake coming here. She missed Colombia's green valleys and mountains. And she was still grieving the death of her younger brother, Arfilio, who had drowned in an accident the previous year. Arfilio had been like her son, and the heartache of his death never subsided.

My father and mother soon fell into a routine. He would leave for work, and my mother would cook dinner for him when he returned. After several months, loneliness led her to be intimate with my father. She started feeling poorly in the spring. She attributed it to nostalgia, missing Colombia, and feeling isolated by a life without friends and only an occasional visit from her sister. When she told Delia she wasn't feeling well, Delia took her to the doctor. She went in thinking it was a virus. Instead, she left with a pregnancy diagnosis.

When she told me her story, we were in the garden weeding her beloved peonies. When she called me over, I thought I'd done something wrong until she said, "I need to tell you something you should know and that I am ashamed of."

"Are you okay?" Concerned, I put down my gardening tools and sat next to her.

"You know, when we came to the United States, your father and I lived together and married later. But we married because I became pregnant with you," she said, bowing her head. "Your spirit demanded a place in this world."

"I don't understand," I replied, confused and anxious.

In a soft voice, her eyes averted and her head bowed, she was more explicit. "I didn't have intercourse with your father. But we got very close. I didn't think I could be pregnant without intercourse, but I was."

My breath caught in my throat as I considered what she was saying. Was this even possible? Still confused, I asked, "What did Daddy say when you told him?"

My mother began to cry as she confessed. Between sobs, she

answered, "He told me it wasn't him because he did not enter me. He told me it was someone else's child. It wasn't."

Despite the gravity of our conversation, I had a wild vision of millions of little semen soldiers crashing the ramparts of my mother's castle and battering down the door to enter the sacristy of her womb, finding the holy grail and taking long, deep sips. Those little fuckers.

At that moment, I was torn between my compassion for her, imagining what it must have felt like to be so alone, and the guilt I felt because I had been the cause of a life of sacrifice that neither she nor my father had signed up for.

"But you got married," I said, wondering if that was even true.

"Yes, Carlo forced your father to marry me, but he said that if I wasn't a virgin on our wedding night, he would leave the next day."

"What happened?" I was now in suspense, as if she were telling someone else's story.

"I spent all afternoon cleaning," she said, looking up with a weak smile, "until there was nothing else to clean. Then I had to go to bed. In the morning, there was blood on the sheets."

She didn't have to explain anything else. I sat with her for a while as she dried her tears. "Why did you wait so long to tell me?"

"Because I wanted you to be old enough to know how much we love you. You came into life in such an unusual way, and I think you should know that. You were destined to be in this life. When you came home from the hospital, your father had a big sign that read, 'Bienvenida, Alicia Margaret Rodriguez.' He loves you and always has."

I remembered seeing a photograph of the kitchen in that apartment with a banner welcoming me. It was in a family photo album my mother kept inside the Magnavox stereo console in the living room.

I never spoke to my father about my mother's confession, but she told him about our conversation. He was upset and worried it would cause a rift in our relationship. But it didn't. What it did was create existential doubt. Why had I been born when the chances were so slim that my conception should happen at all? The feeling I had carried of being an outsider, even as a small child, grew more pronounced after my mother shared her story.

Ever since I can remember, I have felt a deep longing for something ineffable, a connection to the divine that I could feel in every cell of my body and that I would catch glimpses of in dreams and visions. I had always been searching for a way back to that connection. As a child, I cried in church, overwhelmed by a nascent spirituality I could not understand. Napo had reignited that longing for the divine. Shamanism showed me a path for recovering that connection and returning to my place of belonging.

Everyone wants to feel like they belong—to someone or someplace. Belonging is part of our identity. We look for it in our relationships, work, and travels. It defines us. Belonging to a place means sharing the same DNA, history, and values of the land, community, and neighbors. Belonging provides the comfort of not being alone in the world. Being accepted as part of a tribe is elemental to human survival.

We are inherently connected to one another, yet the world is so divided. Perhaps the stranger I meet on the street reflects what is strange in me. A woman and her child remind me of my child and my motherhood status. We find our place of belonging when we look deeply into the eyes of another human being.

Our places of belonging are grounded in love. Each home I have ever had held the bud of love, never reaching its full bloom. I used to believe that love was enough. In some ways, it is, but not in the ways I assumed. Love may help you overcome adversity, but that doesn't mean there's no loss. Love may keep you moving forward, but that doesn't mean you aren't haunted by the past. Fairy-tale endings hide the reality of time passing, ignore the unwritten rules of destiny, and diminish the emotional calving that happens when life chips away at your soul and joy.

As I sit on the dock with Finn on this warm autumn day, my feet dangling into the Chesapeake Bay, I mull over a question: Why am I here? The bay isn't listening; it only sends the vibration of the waves over and over again. A simple question arises as I gaze beyond the horizon: Where did that wave begin?

Where did *my* wave begin? How far in the past was it written that I would meet a shaman who would awaken that source inside me, the one I had searched for since the beginning of my life? How would I find my place of belonging? Or might the answer be here with me now, on this dock, where I belong to the water, to my dog, to my neighbors, to all that is around me, as much as I belong to myself? Belonging not as a place but as divine DNA that I share with all living beings.

This inquiry inspires me to step into the unknown, not simply in search of an answer but to alleviate the feeling of being haunted by a question I do not yet fully understand.

– 8 –

BREAKING THE CHRYSALIS

Between April 2012 and March 2014, I travel back and forth to Ecuador. During that time, Napo and I struggle with the logistics of travel, the legalities of a visa application, and all the emotions that come with a long-distance relationship. I maintain my coaching practice even as I carve out time for those weeks- and sometimes month-long trips.

It feels as if I'm living in two worlds. In one, I work with senior executives in corporate environments across DC, New York, and Boston dressed in my Stuart Weitzman shoes, Italian suits, and Kate Spade purses. In my other world, I walk through rainforests sweating in rubber boots or hugging my backpack as I sit for hours on dirty buses to reach destinations where a twenty-dollar-a-night room means a warm bed but a cold shower and geckos on the walls.

My life becomes one big question to explore. *Why am I here?* I dance between two worlds. I feel like I could belong to both, but I'm confused about why I keep feeling pulled to a country that challenges all my beliefs about how my life should be. I have worked so hard to run a successful and profitable business. Before meeting Napo, I had been happy by anyone's measure. I lived on the Chesapeake Bay, right on the water, in a small community of people who felt like family. I had enough money to buy what I wanted and still invest. Everything pointed to the successful life promised by hard work, perseverance, and education. But now that I've met Napo, I'm drawn to a world opposite everything I wanted to achieve. Why?

I begin to question whether my relationship with Napo will last. Even though I'd purposely kept to myself for years after the divorce, I wonder if it's a rebound from the breakdown of my marriage. I had felt safe when I was hiding from the potential of another heartbreak. I had buried my pain in my work, transforming it into the energy to heal others.

My heart had been sealed, except for those days when I would take out my sleek red sea kayak and spend blissful hours riding waves on the bay. Out there, it was just me and the wind and the water. Ospreys would fly overhead, gracing me with their swoops and dives, triumphantly emerging from the water with fish in their beaks as if to show me that only by diving into dark waters would I ever return.

There is a language that only exists in nature, a tone that heals and embraces the heart by whispering, "Don't worry. You are safe here with me. I will rock you gently and nurture your soul. Pour your salty tears into my waters, and I will heal your wounds." After my divorce, I had poured myself into those waters, like a drop of rain that merges with the vast expanse of the sea, so I could become more than a walking wound. I raced the tides as fast as I could to exhaust myself, purging negativity from my body until I would land on a speck of shore, pull in my kayak, and fall asleep on the sand, dreaming my way back to myself.

The distance between Napo and me sometimes feels like it disappears during our almost daily calls. We spend hours on Skype. We don't just talk about our lives—he also puts on the mentor's mantle as he shares shamanic wisdom lessons with me. In one conversation, I broach the subject of our relationship.

"Did you know that every relationship is destined to fail?" he comments.

That is not what I need to hear. "Then why should we even try, given that everything is against our having a relationship?" I am hurt and angry.

"Relationships fail because they are based on the human mythology of love. Fairy tales we are told as children. The prince rides in to save the princess, and they live happily ever after. There is no substance to that kind of love. It isn't even love. It's a relief—from loneliness, from your thoughts and emotions, from the fear of being alone in this world. We cannot ask that of another person."

That makes sense to me. I see how difficult it is for people I know to be alone. They confuse being alone with being lonely.

Napo continues, "We must be whole unto ourselves first before we are in a relationship with another. We must accept all aspects of ourselves—the light and the shadow, the masculine and the feminine. Love, real love, never comes from outside you. It starts inside, with *amor propio*. This is the love of self that connects us to our divine origin. It is the acknowledgment that the Creator made us more than our human condition, unlimited beings born of the stardust of the universe. When we recognize our divine origin, we see the same in others who reflect our essence. That reflection in another tells us we are alive and present, a vital, creative force beyond our mental limitations."

"I still don't understand why you say relationships are doomed." I notice a kind of pleading in my voice that makes me uncomfortable.

"We seek to become one with our divine nature, and we look to someone else to complete us. It is what Carl Jung called individuation. He could only speak of it in psychological terms. I speak of it in spiritual terms. As each person strives for wholeness, conflict arises. It may appear as not feeling valued by the other partner or resentful that the other is not supporting us somehow. It has less to do with the other person than our feelings about ourselves."

His words cause me to reflect on my failed marriage. I remember those feelings—of not being heard or valued. I remember feeling like a wilting flower, kept alive only by the occasional drops of life-giving water, those random acts of care and love I was so desperate for.

Napo says, "This resentment of not being valued originates in not valuing ourselves enough to meet our needs so we can continue growing and evolving toward wholeness. It means we must enter our basement, where the treasure lies hidden in the shadows. Knowing that every relationship has the imminent potential for destruction makes us pay attention to the quality of that relationship. We must thoughtfully and purposefully serve the relationship to avoid its destruction. What is important is the awareness that the individual drive for wholeness puts us in a position to destroy the very thing we love if we do not understand that our impulse for unity is always present."

"Well then, how do you explain this to someone who has no idea about this dynamic? How do you find a partner you can evolve with?" I have chosen to be in a relationship with Napo because I feel he is that partner for me.

Napo explains, "We must first learn to partner with our opposite within. If I am a woman, I must first engage in a conversation with my masculine aspect. If I am a man, I must engage in a conversation with my feminine aspect. To find the right partner, we must get acquainted with the opposite aspect, nurturing and loving the aspect of ourselves that was diminished when spirit became embodied in a human being with a particular gender." This is another way to describe *amor propio*, one of the basic tenets of shamanism.

He continues, "We must seek the strength that is found in creating harmony within. If you have done the inner work on reconciling your masculine and feminine aspects, you will energetically attract someone who senses this in you. This is why I chose you."

I remember the comment I made about his hands when I first met him. On that evening, we had sat together in Carlos's living room and I had taken his hands in mine. They were delicate, his fingers long and tapered. The bones underneath his soft skin seemed fragile. I had commented that he had a woman's hands. He had felt fully seen at that moment. I had sensed his feminine aspect, something that no one else had recognized in him.

We speak for a while longer, and he concludes the lesson by saying, "This inner harmony generates *amor propio*. There is no need, wanting, or deficiency to fill. You are ready to invite a relationship based on love because you are whole and recognize your divine origin. You are enough."

It isn't long before the lesson on relationships is challenged. During the months when we're apart, we have several exchanges that end in arguments. I won't let go of my attachment to my life and ideals, and he won't compromise or accept that other perspectives might be as valid as his. On the morning of February 18, 2013, Napo calls me when I return home from spending a few weeks in Boston. We hadn't spoken as much as usual while I was away. Now, he's angry and doubts my commitment. That morning, he breaks off our relationship, saying I am immature and unable to comprehend the wisdom he imparts.

My knees buckle under the weight of his words. The air seems to have been sucked out of the room as I fall onto the bed with my iPad, still on the Skype call. I completely disintegrate, overpowered by grief and loss in a way I have never experienced—not even when my father died or my marriage ended. I hadn't had such a response when I began losing my mother to Alzheimer's or when I lost my house in the 2008 financial crash. There were times in my life when it would've been appropriate to break down and not want to get back up. But never, even in the worst times, have I fallen apart so completely or so quickly. I don't recognize myself. I am overwhelmed by an emotional tsunami. I literally think I will die.

I can't stop crying. I can't get out of bed. I can't eat. I can't even take care of Finn, my dog. All day long, I go through a process of disintegration even as my mind fights, telling me, "This is not who I am. This does not happen to me. This cannot happen to me."

Little by little, as daylight fades, the voice disappears until I hear nothing but the sound of my heart and the waves of the bay as they hit the shore rocks outside my apartment. I cry until the darkness of night comes and I surrender to sleep.

The sun's rays always beam into my east-facing room at dawn, and it's like that the next morning. I gradually awaken and hear these words: "Alicia, go to that power of love that lives within you to continue." I write those words down so I won't forget that moment. It's a clear and cold day. I raise the blinds as the sun's rays clear the horizon beyond the bay. Then everything outside dissolves into emptiness. My room doesn't exist anymore. I don't exist anymore. I only feel my presence, without body, without mind, without limit, in profound silence.

At that moment, I finally understand what it is to be alive. I know that no matter what happens, I will continue. I connect with an infinite spiritual life force beyond the body whose source lies in something more numinous than my mortal being. I have experienced a kind of death, and this morning, beckoned back to life by the sun's rays, I've made it to the other side.

It is a direct experience with *amor propio*. Not even the man I love remains at that moment. Not even Alicia remains at that moment. There is nothing but the feeling of being alive, present and whole in a profound, loving silence.

That morning, the chrysalis dissolves and a beautiful butterfly emerges to take flight, knowing her rebirth was worth her suffering, accepting that her death was necessary to live the life she is meant to live.

We suffer when we don't allow the soul's wishes to direct our lives, especially once that soul has awakened. We suffer when we try to hold on to the relationships, youth, material things, and ways of being that no longer serve the soul's desires.

Those who are at peace remain in the flow of life, as if allowing a river's current to take them. No fighting, only a graceful surrender to the shift from matter to spirit. There is a falling away, but there is nothing to replace it. That's what's frightening.

I had learned to be with the void and allow it to empty me so that something sacred could finally appear. That morning, I discover that who I am has nothing to do with the outer world. I finally grasp that I am a soul whose origins come from infinite love. This realization releases me from struggle. It frees me to do and be more than I'd ever believed possible.

− 9 −
SACRED SPACES

When I was in my forties, I signed up for an eight-week course called Awakening. A woman named Jessica led it. She always arrived late, floating into the cavernous barn where classes were held like a heavenly spirit in her long white dress. Her acolytes revered her. I thought it felt like a cult.

During one weekend of the Awakening course, she led us in a deep breathwork experience called Integrative Breathwork. It's an alternative technique where the therapist assists the client in a specific kind of rapid, shallow breathing to help release emotions. To me, it seemed like hyperventilating on purpose to shift into a trancelike state.

One of her assistants, Barbara, was assigned to work with me. Barbara was an average thirtyish-looking woman with short reddish hair, a soft voice, and a pleasant demeanor. I felt safe around her.

I lay on the wooden floor with a pillow under my head and a soft, furry blanket over me. As Barbara's soothing voice merged with the cadence of my breath, I went into a hypnotic state, something I had always found easy to do.

In this trance—which felt like being in a dream—I was swimming in a large, dark cenote in an underground lake. I was relaxed and content. I felt safe and peaceful.

I heard a rhythmic beat, like a soft drum, echoing in the cave in sync with my heartbeat. I swam to the wall and placed my hand against it. Surprisingly, it was warm, soft, and wet, not hard like rock.

Although the cave was predominantly dark, a small but bright light glowed from further inside. I knew my sense of safety and peace came from that light. I decided to swim toward it, and as I did, it became brighter and more expansive. Unconditional love, an ecstatic type of love, filled me as the echo of the beat grew louder. When I am in sacred spaces, I feel that same warmth, love, and safety—what I now call the Beloved, or some call God or the Creator.

Suddenly, the water started to recede, like when the tide goes out of a cave, and the opening to the outside enlarged as the water bled out. The current carried me toward a gap where the light on the other side was too bright and penetrating. I struggled to swim against the current and stay in the cave. I was terrified as I was swept through the opening, and I screamed as I glimpsed the beckoning light one last time.

I woke from the trance disconcerted. Barbara wrapped me in a blanket and held me tightly as I sobbed. That was my birth memory.

My mother used to tell me that I had raging temper tantrums when I was a small child and no one could understand why. I know now that I was angry at being forced into a world I'd never wanted to join. I raged at being extracted from my mother's womb with forceps. Physically, the instrument had damaged my neck, but the existential damage was unseen. I would always feel a yearning, a profound long-ing, to return to that light.

In my twenties, as I traveled the globe, I sought God in imposing cathedrals around the world and in small, humble chapels in European villages and towns. I made it a point to light a candle at each chapel, a kind of pilgrim's offering. By my thirties, I had failed miserably at being a good Catholic. I had become disillusioned by a spirituality that was contaminated by the Church's greed, manipulation, and hypocrisy.

After years of Catholic school, I had become intimidated by religion instead of nourished by it, so much so that during my marriage interview with the head priest of my local church, I even forgot my address. I became catatonic in front of the parish priest, who loomed like a character from the Inquisition. Jerry, my husband-to-be, came to the rescue, casually dropping that his mother had been Catholic Woman of the Year in Portland, Maine. It worked. We were married in the Church, much to the delight of both our mothers.

In 1990, my husband and I lived in Roslindale, a suburb of Boston. Our house was a short distance from the Arnold Arboretum, a 281-acre preserve, an oasis in the Jamaica Plain neighborhood. Its proximity made it easy to visit regularly. This forested place, filled with the scents of evergreen and pine, became my church.

With Brandy, my Irish retriever, I would walk the arboretum's lesser-traveled paths, seeking the little-known spaces, crawling behind bushes to find the circle of light within the tall eastern white pines. That was my cathedral. There, I sought my transcendent aspect—my divine self, a gift from the universal life force that some people call God. Nature was my home base for the search.

Looking back, I can see that I've always found my place of worship in spaces where I feel the divine, where my tears flow unencumbered by judgment, not as a penalty for sins but as a tender wound opens to heal. Throughout my life, I've found my religion in nature's great cathedrals: the Redwood Forest, the Grand Canyon, the cenotes of Mexico, and the rainforests of Ecuador.

I now understand that seeking the divine is the common thread that has followed me throughout my life. It began with my birth and my memory of leaving the sacred in that universal womb where love was the amniotic fluid that nourished the spirit before it incarnated.

To this day, no matter where I am or where I travel, I look for sacred spaces to ground me in that invisible but powerful connection to all of creation. There is beauty and awe in the world's magnificent cathedrals with their stained glass and incense-imbued spaces. In these places, we bow to grandeur created by the hands of man but miss the pain and suffering. It's tucked into the darkness of the confessional box on the side of the altar with its shame, whispers, and benedictions, and it's in the stone foundations laid by people enslaved to a patrimony of division, exclusion, and war.

It is different in the natural world. When birdsongs greet me in the morning, I hear hymns. When sunset rays pierce the clouds, I see what my mother called *la mano de Dios*, God's hand. When I look into a starlit sky from the rainforest in Ecuador, I see a million candles lit in ceremony. And when the full moon calls to me in the early morning hours, I focus on its saintly halo, *la corona*, which defines all that is holy.

How can I ever reconcile the tears of the child kneeling at the pew, ready to receive a blessing at Sunday mass, with the wildness within that revels barefoot in every clear stream and dives beneath the ocean waters to listen for the heartbeat of the Mother womb?

If there has been a quest worth taking, if there have been questions worthy of pursuing, then these that arise in the form of obtuse koans will always drive me forward, searching for the unanswerable.

— 10 —
LOVING THE SHAMAN

After the breakup, Napo reconsiders and we agree that I will travel to Ecuador the following month. We travel to several places he feels I should experience during my visit. First, we visit Tulipe, a rural town a few hours from Quito known for its archaeological complex and museum. As usual, we travel by bus on treacherous roads and stop in small villages along the way.

We arrive in the late morning. There's no sign or any other cues to indicate we've arrived at a bus stop. However, Napo knows where to get off since he has been here before. We jump down from the bus and onto a dusty road, daypacks across our shoulders. To the left is a path that leads to the ruins. Just before it is a long building with a low thatched roof covering an open-air patio with about five plastic tables and chairs. An older man sits at the doorway, staring at us as we pass.

"*Hola*," Napo calls. "Will you be serving lunch today?"

"*Sí, ya pronto*," replies the gray-bearded man. He wears an over-sized shirt and torn pants that scarcely cover his dirt-stained bare feet.

"Okay, *ya volvemos*." Napo promises to return as he guides me onto the gravel path.

Within twenty minutes, we reach Tulipe's main archaeological complex. It's made up of six different structures that resemble pools and are connected by an aqueduct. Spirals and petroglyphs are carved into the walls.

Napo explains that there is an astrological significance to the placement of the pools, which are now empty. "These pools were once filled with water reflecting the night sky, like a celestial map for the shamans to interpret for planting and harvesting," he says.

As we stand on the complex's grassy edges, Napo asks, "Do you see that platform at the center of this long pool?" He points to a long, elevated pathway that splits the largest pool, a circle about thirty feet in diameter, made of gray volcanic rock, with bench-like structures lining its circumference. He says, "This is where the shamans would conduct their ceremonies. Once the shaman had accomplished his time on earth, he would stand on the platform, surrounded by the people, and speak to the cosmos and the earth. He would ask permission from the cosmos for his spirit to return to the Creator, and he would beg Pachamama to release his material being so he could begin his journey home. This ceremony might take several days and nights. Once permission was granted, the shaman would stand on this platform, his arms raised, and disappear, returning to his true home."

"What do you mean, he would disappear?" I ask incredulously.

"His material form would disappear in front of the people, and a new shaman from the community would take his place," he explains.

As he speaks, I envision this area lit by torches, drums beating under a starlit sky, and a man dressed in white clothes adorned with colorful ribbons and long hair tucked under a headdress, chanting into the wind, tears falling from his eyes in supplication to the Creator, asking to return to his home of origin. His chanting would gradually become an echo, and slowly, in the smoky veil of palo santo, the human form would evaporate, leaving only white cloth and an etched rattle lying on the stone.

I turn to Napo, who now stands far from me and faces the platform. He is still, and I feel his presence has drifted elsewhere. He slowly walks over to me, his head bowed. I take his face into my hands and kiss him. The salty tears flowing from his eyes moisten my lips.

His teary eyes speak of a longing, a homesickness, a plea to find his own way home to the Creator. We stand together for several minutes, caught between an ancient time and the present moment. We then turn and walk hand in hand to the road, speaking the language of silence that has always connected us.

We are in Napo's cramped kitchen at his house in Quito. I have made coffee, and he has returned from the bakery down the street with warm bread and rolls. We are sitting at the kitchen table when he announces our next trip. "You must come to our land, Alicia. It's time you understood where we come from and why the land is sacred to us."

"When do we leave?"

Never one to be unclear, he says, "Today."

Without pausing, I finish breakfast, clean the kitchen, and pack a bag. Within an hour, we are on a bus that is headed to Puerto Quito. The Luna family reserve is on the way.

I feel green after two hours of riding a bus that winds around the mountains. I keep my breakfast down by sipping water and munching on stale crackers I find in my backpack. Napo focuses my attention by telling stories and making me laugh.

We stop in Pedro Vicente Maldonado, a small city located at the base of the western cordillera of the Andes as you travel toward the coast. The climate is tropical—a rainforest. Napo gets off the bus to buy lunch and returns with chicken and rice meals. I get off to stretch a bit, feeling cramped by the uncomfortable seats and jolting ride. "We'll eat when we get to Lunahuasi," he says. In translation, this means "House of Luna," and it's the name of the Luna family's property.

Within fifteen minutes, we are back on the crowded bus. We've lost our seats, so we have to stand, carrying our packs and lunch. As the bus comes to a lurching stop, I lose my balance and fall into the lap of an older Ecuadorian man. He doesn't seem to mind as he smiles toothlessly at my apology. Napo nudges me toward the front, indicating the door. There is no formal bus stop. "Why are we getting off in the middle of nowhere?" I ask.

"We are not in the middle of nowhere. We are at Lunahuasi," Napo says as we make our way to the front of the bus and disembark. We climb a steep driveway after lifting the long steel pole that extends across the opening to his land. "The house is up there." He motions toward the top of the hill.

Midway up the hill, three barking dogs come running toward us. One of them, a dog that weighs about fifty pounds and has a spotted coat, goes straight to Napo. As the dog runs toward him, Napo opens his arms, calling, "Manchita!" The dog leaps joyfully into his arms, almost knocking him over, feverishly licking his face and whining from the emotion of the encounter. The other dogs surround Napo, competing for his embrace.

Breathing heavily, we reach the top of the hill. I see a modest house across a patch of land at the top of the driveway. The dogs are still barking playfully when a stocky, dark-skinned man approaches us. He is the caretaker. He shakes Napo's hand.

"Lucho," Napo says, "this is my wife." He says this even though we are not married. "She is American and not used to the rainforest. We will be staying one or two nights. Make sure everything is ready for us."

Lucho's eyes shift from the ground to my face, then back to Napo. "*Sí*, Don Luna," he responds meekly, reminding me of a dog that is afraid of its master. When Napo turns away, Lucho looks at me again, more like a stare. I wonder what he's thinking. My internal voice says, "I don't like this man." I'm uncomfortable around Lucho. There is something untrustworthy about him. His eyes seem to hide secrets. I don't say anything to Napo, but I remain on guard at Lunahuasi.

Lucho picks up our bags and leads us to the house. Inside, it's rustic. The ground floor has two bedrooms, a room for storage, and a main room with a picnic table, a bench, and an old desk against one wall. Taped to the concrete walls are faded photographs alongside newspaper clippings of the shamans conducting ceremonies at the pyramids and elsewhere. Colorful handmade knickknacks sit on the windowsill to brighten the room. A flight of stairs leads to a loft with pristine wooden floorboards and windows overlooking the highway and rainforest. The loft smells of sweet wood and is empty of all furniture.

As someone accustomed to premium hotel rooms, I'm not thrilled to spend the night here. The bedroom has a ceiling fan that blows the mosquito net side to side, and I know I'll be presented with a choice tonight: fan or net. It's muggy and hot, with no breeze. The windows do not have screens. I'm damned either way.

Lucho brings us a five-gallon water bottle as we sit at the picnic table in the main room to eat the lunch Napo picked up. I don't notice my hunger until that first bite of braised chicken. The sweetness of the plantain compliments the spiced rice. I finish eating in minutes.

After lunch, Napo calls Lucho over and asks him to come on a walk around the property to inspect it for upkeep and security. I stay a few steps behind them, surprised by Lunahuasi's expanse and curious about its various plants, trees, and animals. Lucho reports on the maintenance that has been done and also explains what still needs to be done. I can see that Napo isn't happy. The grounds are in disarray. There are broken pipes near the house. The dogs are mangy and look too thin. Several areas are overgrown with thorned brush, and fencing is missing in places.

"What have you been doing?" Napo growls at Lucho. Lucho cowers like a dog waiting to be hit. His eyes focus on the ground. "You haven't been doing anything! This is a mess." I step away, listening to Napo's voice rise in anger. He and Lucho continue walking the grounds. I follow, leaving enough distance between us that I can't hear the conversation. By the tone, I know things are not well.

Sweat drips down my face, and my T-shirt clings to my body. This is the rainforest, a place brimming with life because of the moisture and heat. It feels ancient here. Everywhere I look, something is growing. Bananas, coconuts, cherimoya, jackfruit, and mangoes fall from tree branches. In the distance, I hear strange birdsongs, chickens and ducks squawking, and flies and mosquitos buzzing. Life is at its richest here. I feel the earth's energy through my shoes, blessing me with the same vital force that drives all the life around me.

After about thirty minutes of walking, Lucho and Napo separate. Napo approaches me and takes my hand. We silently walk through the grove of fruit trees toward the house. Even as my mind is still, the air is full of movement and life. Birds screech in the trees, and insects buzz in the air. Looking down, I notice a parade of ants dutifully carrying leaves and tiny pieces of fruit to their mound. *So orderly*, I think. *So determined.*

Napo calls Carlos when we arrive at the house, explaining that they will soon need another caretaker. This one is abusive, he says, and is not taking care of the animals or property. I quietly slip outside, uncomfortable with the conversation.

From the front of the house, I look across the street into a vast green expanse of trees. We are up high, so the view extends for miles. This is the rainforest, a carpet of deep green that covers valleys and hills with color, sound, and textures. How random yet meticulous it all seems. There's an order or plan behind the seeming arbitrariness of trees growing at will. It reminds me of the ants I saw marching. The trees are connected by an underground network of roots, and the insects play their part by moving nutrients around. The birds support the system with their ability to pollinate when they move between land and air. The monkeys drop fruit seeds and pits onto the fertile ground. Everything appears chaotic but is deceptively in sync, like a giant natural symphony of life, every creature playing its part to maintain the balance. I have never seen such raw beauty, primitive in its appearance yet intelligent in its harmonious system.

Napo comes outside and announces, "It's time I took you into the rainforest. We won't go too far because you didn't take the malaria pills. I'll take you as far as Vicente's land and the river, but no further."

Vicente is Napo and Carlos's older brother. The Luna brothers each own a piece of the reserve, but they consider it family property. Vicente's property borders the river that creates a boundary between their land and the virgin rainforest. We cross the highway and enter through a small gate on the other side.

Despite the heat, it is necessary to wear long sleeves, long pants, and rubber boots as protection. Napo tells me the rainforest is a dangerous beauty, teeming with all kinds of wondrous creatures and flora—but also deadly snakes, poisonous plants, and microorganisms that can make people very ill. He grew up here, so he is knowledgeable of and immune to bacteria that could make me sick. I follow his instructions knowing I can enjoy the rainforest and be safe.

After passing through the gate, we enter a path I had spied when I was at the house earlier, looking down from above. Napo's machete cuts through the branches and fronds that insert themselves onto the trail. We don't say much. I am busy trying not to slip in the mud, and he seems to be in his own reverie as he leads, perhaps remembering his many previous walks here.

We have been walking for about thirty minutes when Napo stops abruptly. As I approach, I see what he does. Lying before us is a large swath of land full of tree trunks. Someone has cut down the trees, leaving this scene of devastation, an open wound on the land. Everywhere I look, there are crushed plants and deep cuts in the earth, exposing tree roots like veins sticking out of the ground. The trees have been sawed down, leaving stumps like amputated fingers. Napo drops onto a tree trunk and says nothing for a few minutes.

"This piece of land must've been sold to someone. Who would come and destroy our rainforest? Who would destroy our home and the home of all our creatures?" He shakes his head and tries to make sense of the scene before him. Later, I'll learn that poachers often forge sale documents in Ecuador. I'll also discover that the Luna brothers co-own the property with their cousins, who could have illegally sold the land.

"I can't stay here," Napo says. "Let's keep going. It's not far to the river."

We climb around stumps and over trees lying on the ground until we once again enter the rainforest's green canopy. After another twenty minutes, I hear flowing water. We continue toward the sound.

Breaking through the trees, we arrive at the riverbank. The water flows rapidly, dancing around large boulders and fallen branches. Nearby is an inlet where the water pools, making a small beach. We go to the beach together. Napo walks into the cloudy water. I can't see the bottom as we wade in. "Don't go any deeper. Don't get water in your boots." His voice is stern with caution.

He ventures deeper into the flow between the inlet and the river. He wears his cap backward, and sweat plasters his long, wavy hair to his forehead. I can see the outline of his chest through his shirt, which is now wet from the exertion of our walk and the humid climate. He slowly reaches down to touch the water, allowing it to flow between his fingers.

There is something sacred about watching him stand there with the water flowing around him, bent over reverently as if blessing himself with holy water. This is his church, and nature is his religion. We have that in common. Tears stream from his eyes and merge with the river, a part of him going home to a time when, as a child, he swam here. Around us, a chorus of creatures sings a hymn to the Creator. I, as witness, bow my head and begin to cry, feeling a tremendous but unknown loss. We stand apart but also together, our hearts in communion with the heartbeat of the rainforest. Time stands still.

I don't know how long we stand at the river, each of us remembering something ancient, feeling an undefinable longing. Eventually, he reaches for my hand as we climb onto the riverbank and sit on a large boulder.

Napo reminisces about his childhood and growing up in the rainforest. "As a child, I would swim here. The river ran clear then. You could see the tiny fish, the colored pebbles, and the small frogs that would swim in these waters. We would try to catch them and then throw them back in. The river is sick now. No one should swim in it. It used to be larger and fuller. Now it is more like a stream than a river."

The light has changed, and the sun is dropping lower in the sky. "It's time to return," he says. We walk back the same way, going through the stripped land, hitting the road, and crossing to his property. By the time we arrive, my clothes cling to me, soaked with sweat and humidity. There's a cooler breeze now, chilling me despite the heat from my body.

About thirty minutes later, Lucho meets us at the house. His wife has prepared an early dinner of *seco de pollo* (braised chicken), yucca, rice, and plantains, a typical meal in rural areas. I crave a cold beer and am surprised when Napo takes two bottles from the old refrigerator in the spare room. We eat at the wooden dining room table and finish another beer outside as the sun sets.

Before we go to bed, we sit outside under a dark sky brimming with starlight while tiny creatures serenade us. I have never seen a sky like this. It is like looking at infinity, peering through time at faraway galaxies while the stars sparkle like Christmas lights.

I develop a deeper understanding of Napo during this trip. Like these rainforest creatures, he is part of a natural web of life that doesn't tolerate illusion or wishful thinking. Like the creatures of the rainforest, he cannot appease his discomfort with material things and instead must seek its source in something beyond himself.

Everything here is real and raw, connected to all that is in the ground, in the air, in the water, and in the sky. I feel limitless here. If I could only get out of my own way, I might also be privy to an infinite and ancient wisdom that forms the foundation of what it means to be alive. In the rainforest, I feel that vital energy within me and all things. Here, I am confronted with the disturbing realization that the life I have been leading is an illusion. I am here, in this encounter, with this shaman, in the womb of life itself, to learn the truth of who I am and what is real.

– II –
FIRE DREAMS

The dream is the liberation of the spirit from the pressure of external nature, a detachment of the soul from the fetters of matter.

—Sigmund Freud, *The Interpretation of Dreams*

How do you find the truth of your life when your mind blocks it? Carl Jung claimed that dreams are how the unconscious expresses itself. Through the stories told in the dream state, we air our deepest grievances, resolve our humiliations, and engage that which we reject in ourselves. We fight the demons we dare not challenge in the light of day. What has been repressed surfaces in the void, demanding penance for sins committed.

In dreamtime, there is no time or space. There are no agendas, schedules, laws of physics, time continuums, or emotional holdbacks. I'm convinced we dream the same dream, or versions of the same dream, until whatever is lying in the darkness is excavated and brought into the light, transforming reality to create a balance between what is real and what is imagined.

I've always heeded my dreams. I was raised to consider them a natural expression of the soul and its wants and needs. I taught myself lucid dreaming. I'll be in the cinema of sleep, watching myself on the big screen of my mind. I might even notice my running commentary: "Why the hell did I do that?" or "Don't believe him!" or maybe "Don't open that door!" And, of course, I open the door.

One recurring dream I'd had since college turned out to be a lesson I finally learned thirty years later.

In the dream, I was in my twenties and lived in Watertown in the house where I'd grown up. It was a modest house perched at the top of a hill, built in the 1930s and renovated a few times before and during our time there.

In my dream, the house was on fire, and I screamed to my brother and sister to run outside. I frantically searched for my mother and found her behind her bed, crouched down like a child. "Mina, I've got you!" I yelled, calling her by her first name, as my siblings and I always did. I grabbed her, wrapped her in the bright orange shawl she'd always loved, and ran toward the front door through flames and smoke. I could see that my brother and sister were already in the street. I arrived at the door with my mother in my arms. My sister ran to the door as I pushed my mother outside and into my sister's arms, and then . . . I just stood there.

My sister looked at me with disbelief and yelled, "Run, Alicia!" All I could do was stand in the doorway with the flames reaching their long, fiery fingers toward me, the heat toasting my legs and arms.

I knew I had to leave, but I couldn't move. I watched the outside world fade away as I receded into the house, consumed by the flames. Then I'd wake up.

In the dream, I couldn't save myself. I wouldn't save myself. I made sure everyone was out of danger before going back and disappearing.

I'm sure Freud would have a lot to say about this dream. But there's no need. I finally deciphered it much later in life. I always felt that my life was constantly in danger—if not physically, then certainly metaphysically. I have always felt like an outsider looking in, hiding, as my mother had taught me in kindergarten, so no one would know how strange I was. I was sure whoever dropped me off on this planet had made a mistake.

Both in the dream and in my life, I always ensured that those around me were safe and protected before returning to the flames (whether real or metaphorical). It seemed that with every episode, there was a purification; something else was burned in the blaze, something ancestral that I couldn't explain. Perhaps it was a kind of karma—each time, I had to return to the fire for further purification. Each time, an alchemical response purified and molded me in ways I couldn't predict. Each time, I met the fire without flinching, knowing there was more to transmute, as if I were seeking my personal philosopher's stone to transform all the suffering and darkness into the vital energy of an enlightened life.

My time in Ecuador would be the ultimate trial by fire, taking me to the depths of darkness in worlds unknown to me, then raising me like a phoenix to a new sense of being that had lain hidden from the time I entered this world, or perhaps even before that.

— 12 —
THE BEST-LAID PLANS

Napo decides to come to the United States and apply for residency during my trip to see him in March 2013. I didn't ask him to live in the States. He's made it clear he has no desire to live in a culture so disconnected from the natural world and void of genuine spirituality.

Before I knew him, the government had denied Napo entry to the United States. I'd assisted Carlos in writing a letter petitioning for Napo to visit the United States under a special cultural status. That application was unsuccessful.

Once Napo tells me he will come to the United States, I begin researching how to bring him. One of the most coveted documents in the world is a United States green card. As a result, the federal government makes it as difficult as humanly possible to apply for and be awarded this ten-year permanent residency. Because I have little tolerance for bureaucracy, I'm amazed that I follow the complex protocol.

I engage a professional facilitator who tells me that if the government denies Napo's application again, there will be no future opportunities to apply. There is only one way to bring him to the United States: a fiancé visa.

"What does that mean exactly?" I ask the facilitator.

"If he comes on a fiancé visa, you have to get married within ninety days. If you're not married, he'll be forced to leave the country, and most likely he won't be allowed in again."

I tighten my grip on the phone. "What else?" I ask tentatively.

"You have to prove your relationship is genuine. That means preparing hundreds of documents, including emails, phone records, family photos, and airline tickets to show you've been traveling back and forth. And I'm sure there will be other hoops to jump through. It's intrusive, and there's no guarantee they'll allow him to come, even on a fiancé visa."

I notice I'm holding my breath. I finally exhale loudly. "Then what happens?" I ask.

"Once you marry, you'll apply for the resident card. However, getting a green card could take a year or more, and you'll need to budget at least three thousand dollars for the entire process with no guarantee that the attempt will succeed. Are you prepared to do this?"

I hadn't anticipated the seriousness of this process. I'd planned to have Napo visit. I thought we could live together for a bit to see if it would work out. Then we could proceed from there. I've never intended nor desired to remarry. And still, I know that continuing our relationship will be impossible unless he comes to the United States.

We decide to apply for a fiancé visa. I convince myself that I still have a way out. We will have ninety days to see if things work. If they don't, he will return to Ecuador, both of us knowing the relationship is unsuitable. That is my plan. It will fail miserably.

For months, I devote hours a day to completing the requirements. The process is intrusive—and expensive. The government wants all kinds of personal information, including emails and text messages. I also include photographs and airline tickets from my many visits to Ecuador. After months of sorting the necessary materials, I put everything into a package that I send to my facilitator. Then there is one more hurdle—an interview in Guayaquil, Ecuador, at the immigration office.

I fly to Ecuador in November 2013, and we reserve a hotel room for the night before and the night of our November 26 interview. We try to be optimistic. We never say out loud that the second night will either be a disappointment or a celebration; we do not want to travel high on emotion.

The immigration office has fluorescent lights in the waiting room, making everyone's skin look corpse-like. About a dozen couples huddle in their black plastic chairs, whispering anxiously. The place smells of fear and hope mixed into a stank perfume.

We find two chairs together in the middle of the room. Dimmed glass cubicles line one wall, reminding me of confessionals in churches. Behind the glass are uniformed interviewers, their faces blank as they ask questions in Spanish and English. One couple nervously holds hands. She cries and he pleads with the blank face behind the glass. Another visa is denied.

We dare not speak above a whisper. "Do you think they are recording us on video?" Napo asks nervously. I have never seen him feel doubtful about anything.

"We just need to breathe and relax, knowing we have done every-thing correctly. We will be fine," I respond, appeasing my own worry as much as his.

Our thirty-minute wait seems interminable. Then, finally, a disembodied voice calls our names and instructs us to approach a numbered window. We glance at one another. "Breathe, Napo, and only answer the question," I say. "Don't elaborate." I worry he will be long-winded, as is his nature.

We shuffle to the window arm in arm. Standing behind it is a young woman who must be in her twenties. Her face is porcelain white framed by dull brown hair that pokes out of her uniform's cap. Her eyes are expressionless and focused on the paperwork. After a few seconds, she looks at us and asks in Spanish, "Names?"

There is a heaviness in my stomach that feels like I'm holding on to a rock. I remind myself to breathe as I give our names. She con-tinues to ask questions, sometimes directly to one of us, sometimes to the other, and sometimes to both of us. A trickle of sweat runs down my back. I hold on to Napo's arm so I won't shake. Finally, she stops shuffling papers and looks right at us, saying nothing. My heart pounds so hard I think it will explode. Napo's grip on my hand is painful.

"You are approved," the woman says. Her words float through the glass.

"Excuse me?" I ask, unsure if I've heard correctly.

"You are approved for your fiancé visa," she restates in Spanish. Napo grabs me and plants a huge kiss on my lips, oblivious to anyone around us. When I turn to look at the woman, her impassivity has surprisingly transformed into a bright smile. "Good luck to both of you," she says, winking.

We skip back to the hotel like two children. Once we're in the room, I burst into tears. All the months of work and hope had collided in that moment of approval, and now the torrent of emotions overcomes me.

"I am going to the United States, Panterita!" he says like a child who has been granted his biggest wish.

"Yes, Napo, our new life together will begin now," I respond, equally joyful.

On March 2, 2014, during the deepest part of winter, Napo arrives in Maryland with nothing but a small suitcase and the parka I bought him since he has no winter clothes. Because he has never flown internationally, I go to Ecuador earlier in the week and return to the United States with him. He is afraid of flying. Besides that, he does not speak English and has never navigated airports.

It is an uneventful flight with a stop in Miami, where I introduce him to Cuban food. He is delighted to have a meal like what he would eat in Ecuador. After a long layover, we continue the final leg to Baltimore, arriving at midnight. My car is at the airport garage, where

I left it when I flew to Ecuador. We drive to Annapolis and, without even opening our bags, go to bed. We sleep until late the following day.

I live in a small apartment on the Chesapeake Bay in a house that was renovated into four units. I live on the top floor with windows that look out onto the bay. Below me lives a retired army couple, Alina and Steve, whom I have grown fond of. Alina is a Cuban American spitfire, short in stature but with a considerable presence. If you cross her, she'll slice you into tiny pieces with her Cuban swearing. She is fiercely loyal and a total badass. Steve is a quiet and strong presence in the community, a straight shooter who hides his kind heart behind a military veneer. They are the unspoken leaders of the apartment community we affectionately call the Compound. They are also family to me.

I've told them about Napo, and they are anxious to meet him. I feel like I'm taking a new boyfriend to my parents' house for approval. I know that sounds strange as I'm an adult woman, but I want them to like him so he can become part of my Bay family. The day after we arrive in the United States, I take him downstairs to meet them. Alina speaks to Napo in Spanish, which makes him feel more at home. Steve handles the hospitality part of the visit, providing drinks and snacks as we chat about life in Ecuador and here in the United States.

I don't sense their worry, but months later, Steve tells me they were concerned for me that day. They detect what I've missed. I am so blinded by my love for Napo and my dream of living in Ecuador that I miss the red flags that kept appearing while we live at the Compound.

Our wedding date is set for March 31. It will be a simple civil ceremony at the Annapolis courthouse. Later, I'll recognize "ceremony" as a misnomer; it's more of a transaction.

I feel uneasy but ignore it. Napo doesn't want to wait ninety days—he wants to get married as soon as possible. I question this.

We're sitting in the living room talking, he on the sofa and me in an armchair. "Don't you think we should wait a bit longer to see if you feel comfortable in the American culture?" I ask. "You have never liked anything about America except for the fact that your brother lives here. Maybe we should spend more time getting you accustomed to life here before we take this final step?"

Annoyed, he answers, "What is there to wait for? I am here now. That is what I came here for." He stiffens and his face changes into something stonelike.

"You haven't met my friends or family. And I have to go to my office to work every day. You won't see me all day, maybe not until very late. This is the way it is here. I'm just not sure you are going to adapt."

His voice rises. "Adapt? I will not adapt to a life without time or attention to what is spiritual. That is the problem here. No, we will make our own time and our own life. We don't need the rest."

"That's not realistic, Napo. I must work, or we don't have money. My hours during the day are for work. You'll have to find employment and something to do with your time while you're here." I match his annoyance with my frustration.

He rises abruptly, his face blossoming into a red ball of fury as he flies to my chair and hovers above me. "You will not dictate to me what I will do here. I have my plans. We are together now and will decide how to manage life here and in Ecuador. I will not stay in the United States all the time. You will not either. It's time you understood what this is. There is only us now. No one else to trust." He marches toward the front door and angrily leaves the apartment. I'm left wondering what happened, shocked at his anger and confused about what he meant by "no one else to trust."

A few hours later, he returns. He only says, "Make the appointment for the marriage as soon as possible. We will not talk more about this."

We do not invite anyone to the wedding and only tell a few people. Carlos refuses to come, and Napo doesn't want anyone else to be there. We schedule the civil ceremony for three o'clock in the afternoon. Alina volunteers to be our witness and take photographs. Although it is sunny and still, it's cold enough that the air bites into my lungs.

Napo wears the black leather jacket I bought him, pairing it with an Ecuadorian wool scarf that he wraps around his neck. Under his jacket, he wears a white shirt, a blue sweater, and his only pair of nice pants. He also wears the formal black shoes I bought him a few weeks earlier just for this occasion. He rarely wears anything other than jeans, T-shirts, sneakers, and, in the winter, the brown parka I gave him when he arrived.

I look more like I am going to a funeral than a wedding. I'm dressed in a black turtleneck sweater under a black wool coat with black leggings fitted into black boots. I will later wonder if a wiser, more conscious aspect of myself was sending me clues as to what I really felt about that day.

I resist the voice that tells me to run. I am being pushed into a current that I can't stop. The best I can do is lie back and allow it to take me without bashing my head against the river's boulders. The noise of the rushing water and the need to keep breathing drown out the small screaming voice telling me my life does not depend on this extraordinary relationship.

Upon arriving at the courthouse office, we meet a tall older woman with an efficient demeanor and rust-colored hair wrapped tightly in a bun. After we've completed some paperwork, she brings us into another room. She looks directly at me when she asks, "Do you both take the promise of this marriage of your own free will and under no duress?"

Silencing the screaming voice, I reply, "Yes."

Throughout the ceremony, she keeps her eyes focused on me.

Later, I will recognize that she is giving me a way out. I keep saying "yes." We are married within fifteen minutes.

There is no celebration, no congratulations, no joy. This transaction has set the trajectory of my life. I will be on this path until I can finally allow that oppressed voice to break through.

− 13 −
LIFE ON THE CHESAPEAKE BAY

You may wonder why I married Napo despite hearing the voice within telling me to run, that something was wrong. I've wondered the same thing. It has taken years to disentangle the reasons I allowed this relationship to develop and continue to the point where I felt something terrible would occur if I left.

After years of therapy and much soul-searching, I finally understand a few things I'd like to say are untrue. But it appears that may not be so.

Somewhere in my life, I began to associate love with suffering. I only knew I was in love if I was suffering. Love and pain were two sides of the same coin. When I look back on my relationships, each one has an element of bittersweetness. My relationship with Napo was also not the first time I had fallen in love with someone and moved for him. I met a young Norwegian man when, in my twenties, I was hired as a tour guide for a group going to Scandinavia. His name was Erik, and he was the local tour guide. During the fourteen-day tour, Erik and I became the "young couple in love," as those in the group dubbed us. The tourists were older, and we reminded them of what it was to be young and romantic.

After the trip, Erik showed up unannounced on my doorstep in Boston, where I was living with my family. My mother, always the wise one, immediately disliked him. He stayed with a friend of a friend. Eventually, he convinced me to move to Colorado with him. The thought of an adventure with this charismatic man enthralled me. I was young and foolish, only seeing the move as an extension of the Scandinavia trip. My departure broke my mother's heart. She knew it was the wrong move for me. A year later, I returned disconsolate and emaciated from the stress of being far from home with a man I discovered was not the person I had met in Norway. Erik had disappeared one day, returning to Norway. I had refused to marry him, so he could not remain in the United States. I never heard from him again.

The only significant healthy relationship I'd experienced was with my ex-husband. Jerry was and still is a man of integrity, kindness, and intelligence. However, years of loss took their toll on our marriage. He became distant, and as we tried to survive our many wounds, we lost the connection that had anchored us. Nevertheless, we are friends to this day and work together as loving parents to Joseph, our son. Time has transformed our relationship into a deep and respectful affection.

The winter of 2014 is bitterly cold. Relentless wind on the Chesapeake Bay seeps through the windows and makes me wonder if I will ever be warm again. Napo has never experienced winter. He is both fascinated and appalled by it. "It's so cold here! But it's so beautiful too," he exclaims, trying to manage what he perceives as a contradiction. It isn't until May that the bay comes back to life after the deep freeze.

We develop a weekday routine that helps Napo adjust to life in the United States, allowing me to run my business from an office in Annapolis. In the mornings, I take him to Carlos's house and he spends the day there. The brothers enjoy working out later in the day. I meet Napo at the gym, and then we drive home. I usually cook, and after dinner, we walk in the woods with my dog, Finn, near Sandy Point Park.

Once summer arrives, the Compound comes to life. Most evenings, we sit outside with Alina, Steve, and others who live here, enjoying snacks or cocktails by the firepit. Napo begins having difficulty socializing, not only because he doesn't speak English but also because he has always been a loner. He prefers that we keep to ourselves.

"Everyone is too involved in our lives, Alicia. I don't like it," he complains one day. "It becomes dangerous when the lives of others and their opinions and ways intrude into our life."

"They are my friends, Napo, and my life is intertwined with theirs," I respond defensively. "I relax when I'm with them. We laugh, and the stress of the day leaves my body. They are like family to me."

His displeasure grows in the summer months. It doesn't occur to me that he's trying to isolate me. I attribute his attitude to his difficulty adjusting to a different culture and lifestyle. He begins to drink more, and to limit his drinking, I often leave the group earlier than I normally would.

At the end of August, the Compound throws a party. Family members and friends join residents to share food, drinks, and fun in the pool. Napo stands on the upper terrace area, holding his beer and observing the crowd. He looks confused and unhappy. "Why don't people dance here? There is music, but no one is dancing. Everyone is just talking and talking too much."

"Everyone is enjoying themselves, Napo. Maybe later people will dance, but you can see people are having fun in the pool and laughing. Let's go down and join them." I nudge him toward the crowd and grab his hand. "There's more food, too, if you're still hungry," I say, thinking that might be a good strategy.

We approach the bar where Steve, acting as bartender, invites Napo to try a cocktail. "You'll like this, Napo. It's a bit strong. It's called a mojito, and it's from Cuba, like Alina." We all laugh as Steve mixes the drink and hands it to Napo. I hold my breath, hoping this might help him relax.

He purses his lips after a sip, then breaks into a smile. "I like this,

Steve!" Napo exclaims in English. He finally relaxes and, with halting English, joins the conversation.

I don't count how many drinks he has that night. It is past midnight when we go upstairs to my apartment. He slurs his words and is unsteady on his feet. "How many drinks did you have?" I ask, concern in my voice.

"It doesn't matter," he responds, annoyed at the question.

Once inside the apartment, he turns abruptly to me and demands, "Where were you? I saw you left the party. Where did you go?"

"I'm not sure what you mean when you say I left the party. The only time I left was to come to the apartment and go to the bathroom." I'm surprised at his tone and sense an aggression I don't recognize.

"You left when Steve left," he says accusingly. "Where were you two?" He moves toward me, blocking the door and causing me to back into the wall. "Where were you?" he yells into my face.

I put my hands up defensively as his body begins leaning into mine. "Stop! What are you doing?" Then he pushes me against the wall. There is a rushing sound in my ears as his words echo. Then I push him away from me as hard as I can. His face turns red with rage.

"Don't fucking touch me!" I yell at him, knowing the music outside will drown out my words. My body vibrates with a ferocity I recognize as ancient and familiar. Every aggression from every relationship I've ever had surfaces at that moment. "Do not fucking touch me!" I repeat.

I grab my keys and run down the stairs to my car. As I pull out of the driveway, I see him descending the stairs after me. I stop and burst into tears once the Compound is out of sight, my body still shaking from the encounter. "What the fuck?" I keep repeating. I'm confused, disoriented, and sad. I do not recognize the man who yelled at me in the apartment. How could this be the same man I fell in love with? Who is this person?

I drive to my office, prepared to spend the night on my couch. I can't sleep. Whenever I close my eyes, I see Napo's eyes full of rage and jealousy. Unanswered questions ring in my mind. What have I done? Who is this person I married? What will I do now?

I eventually cry myself to sleep, then wake at dawn a few hours later. In the bathroom, I wash my face and question my reflection in the mirror. "What are you going to do now?"

I drive to the Compound, where everyone is sleeping off the effects of last night's party. When I enter, Napo is slumped on the sofa with a drink in his hand. He has been drinking all night and is mostly incoherent.

"I am so sorry, Alicia. I am so sorry," he moans, his face wet with tears. "I love you. I can't bear to see you with anyone. It reminds me of my last love, and she left me." His words are barely understandable through the slurring. He continues talking, collapsed on the sofa, sometimes crying like a child and other times raging like a hurt animal.

The small living room is filled with a toxic energy I have never felt before. It smells of death. I am done. Quietly, I pack a duffel bag with some of his clothes. "I am taking you to your brother's house. I don't want to see you again," I say.

He allows me to lead him out of the apartment, down the stairs, and into the car. I drive the fifteen minutes to Carlos's house, focusing on the road and trying not to shake. He continues crying and raging until, at last, we arrive. I open the car door and, without helping him out, march to the door. "Here is your brother. Keep him!" I say as I throw the duffel bag onto the porch. Carlos looks surprised when he sees Napo stumbling down the path to the house.

"Brother," Napo calls. "Look at what she has done to me!"

Carlos runs down the path to him and helps him walk the distance to the porch, up the stairs, and through the door. I don't wait. I leave as soon as I drop the duffel bag. It will be weeks before Napo and I talk or see each other again.

* *

I am sitting at the bar when I notice three men watching me. They look like brothers with similar features. I am alone, nursing a drink. Dance music is playing, and I notice a man on the floor with several women. He is tall, bulky, and bald. His shirt is tight, revealing a muscular body. He dances well. Dark eyes punctuate his face, reminding me of how owls can look right through you, concealing whatever secret knowledge they may hold of the night.

As the song finishes, the man approaches and asks me to dance. I am hesitant, but he takes my arm and I don't resist. He leads me to the dance floor, and we dance with our bodies close together. Electricity emanates from his body. His presence consumes me. The room blurs, and a feeling of weightlessness overcomes me. Am I dancing or flying? He speaks to me, but I can't hear his words. The music is too loud, and the room is full of sparks of light.

He leads me back to my barstool, thanks me, and returns to the dance floor with three other women. I feel like I am in a trance. My drink tastes bitter on my lips, but it revives my mind. That's when I notice the three men from my earlier observation approaching.

"We are here to warn you," one of them says. "The man that danced with you is dangerous. He will entice you with words and seduce you with energy you have never felt before. You must not listen when he sings to you. You must close your ears and eyes and listen only to yourself."

The man speaks with an accent I don't recognize. "I don't understand. Who are you? Why are you telling me this?" I turn on the barstool to face them. They appear genuinely concerned, but I am cautious.

"The man you danced with is a shaman. We know him. He is dangerous," says another man. "We have come to tell you in a place where you may listen. You have heard us speak before, but you have ignored us. We are here now so you may see and hear us and take our advice. You must leave him. He is powerful, and he will win your soul."

I glance at the dance floor and notice the man I had danced with looking in our direction. He scowls even as he holds one of the women's hands.

When I look back, the three men have disappeared. Then I look back toward the dance floor. The shaman is approaching.

Then I wake up. The dream had seemed so real. My body shakes and I start to cry, remembering the morning when I took Napo to Carlos's house. We have not spoken in weeks. What kind of warning had my dream imparted? Were the men my guides, coming only in dreamtime, when the mind is asleep and unable to rationalize? I'm not sure. I keep this in mind and write the dream in my journal so I won't forget it.

Ultimately, I do not heed the warning. For a time, I lose my soul to the shaman. But in doing so, I learn to rise more resilient than before. Napo awakens my inner spiritual warrior. During my time with him, these three guides travel alongside me, and when I need them most, they return in dreamtime, bearing the gifts of courage, wisdom, love, and resilience. They pick me up when I fall, until finally, I rise and leave.

− 14 −
SEASONS OF LIFE AND DEATH

Tras el movimiento de la totalidad, la unidad que está partida
se nucleariza para tomar conciencia universal.

—Napo

Following the the movement of the totality (oneness/unity), the
singularity (one/individual) that is divided will merge back into
the totality to reach universal consciousness.

There is a dance between life and death that is constant and unseen. Every moment passes and is renewed. Every cell in your body is in a state of dying and regenerating. Your thoughts may direct your life in a specific way in your twenties and later die in the face of new experiences and challenges. The earth spins on its axis and travels around the sun as our galaxy births new stars while others are shattered. We are in constant movement on many levels. What the shamans call *el movimiento universal*—the universal movement—defines the very nature of life, circular and iterative, intuitive and sensing. This is a fundamental principle in shamanism. Shamans don't fear death because they view it as a portal or transition from one form of energy into another. From this perspective, death is only the reflection of life, as if you are looking in the mirror: you are here and your image is there; both you and your image are real and present at that exact moment.

Before I understood this, death was something to avoid and fear. It was the big unknown, darkness made of nothingness. Some people believe that nothing happens after death. Others are taught through religion to believe in life after death, heaven and hell, glory or eternal suffering. Others have seen death up close—war veterans, medical professionals, hospice workers, and those of us who have been present at the death of a loved one. People deal with death according to their experiences, upbringing, and beliefs.

Shamanism knows no social bounds or constraints. It looks to the natural world and sees life and death as cyclical, neither good nor bad. The living cycle, which renews itself, integrates death. This concept is more familiar in cultures that are still developing. The presence of the natural world constantly surrounds these people. Technology, grandiose projects, and busy lifestyles do not absorb their attention. They live close to nature and the earth, and they live according to the natural cycles of life, which more advanced cultures try to manipulate or conquer. Yes, death is everywhere, even when we don't notice. Death stands at your shoulder, whispering, "Be very afraid." It motivates us to do things that bring death nearer, like overworking ourselves, abusing substances, becoming narcissistic or greedy, and abusing power.

But what happens when you meet death up close? Do you accept death's hand, the invitation to a silent and painless world? Or do you remember all the things that make life worth living? I was confronted with that question on a stormy summer night in 2009.

It was summer in Maine, but you wouldn't have known it. The wind blew through Peaks Island as if it were on a mission to knock the little isle off the planet. Peaks Island is situated in Casco Bay, three miles and a twenty-minute ferry ride from Portland, and it was the site of our July escape. My husband's family was from Portland, and our July 4 celebration brought everyone to the island for the yearly barbeque and stories—and the occasional spats that all families experience.

Jerry and I arrived earlier than usual in 2009, in late June, and the weather had not yet caught up to the season. It was cold and blustery in that Maine way that made your nose red, your ears hurt, and your body ache from the damp cold. The overcast sky looked like a dirty pane of glass that had been forgotten long ago. Casco Bay fought the car ferry as it made its way from the mainland to the island, the cars swaying back and forth despite the constraints against their tires. Even our usual stop on Commercial Street for beer and a lobster roll, an event that gleefully screamed vacation, was overshadowed by the pain in my body and soul.

I was physically and emotionally struggling. As my mother used to say, our chapters come in seven-year increments. I was reeling from so many losses and wasn't even close to the end of my seven years. I didn't think I could take anymore.

That summer, I almost ended my story on the rocky shore of Peaks Island. The stress of building a business during a recession, the many losses and constant upheavals, the growing distance in my relationship with Jerry, and the feeling that I was alone and solely responsible for my family took its toll on me. The emotional pain became physical pain. It was excruciating.

Although I saw doctors and they ordered tests, they could find nothing wrong with me. The hypothesis that I was suffering from fibromyalgia merely meant they couldn't determine what was happening. But the pain was indisputable.

After a few days on Peaks, suffering the dark days and the cold, rainy nights, I became overwhelmed. I couldn't think. The pain in my body took over completely.

On the fourth day, I decided to walk in the early evening. It was still light when I left, and there was only a slight drizzle. I felt like I couldn't breathe in the house. Being with my sister- and brother-in-law was exhausting, trying to keep up a facade that Jerry and I were fine. We weren't.

Peaks Island is compact. It's a 740-acre island, so you can walk to any destination, whether by crossing through the middle or taking the shoreline, which is only four miles. I took the shore route to be near the ocean. About an hour into my walk, it started getting dark and began to rain. I turned back toward the house but didn't make it before the rain became a storm, the wind whipping me from all sides and the deluge thoroughly soaking me.

The 8th Maine Regiment Lodge and Museum was located within a mile of the house, and I was close enough that I could seek shelter there. I huddled on the open deck area, sitting at a picnic table to watch the storm. I was soaked through and through. The pain in my body was so intense that I wanted to scream, but no one would've heard me in the raging storm.

A strange calm overcame me as I peered through the mist at the crashing waves. It was as if I had left my body and was hovering above myself. Suddenly, I couldn't feel the rain, cold, or pain. Each wave became an invitation to come closer to the ocean, as if sirens were calling me from beyond the darkness.

I walked down from the deck and toward the rocks hanging over the turbulent waters. I couldn't feel the biting rain anymore, only the wind pushing me closer to the ocean. My eyes focused on the water, my legs moving stiffly, I walked like a zombie.

The edge of the cliff came closer and closer. A voice insisted, "One more step, one more step, and you'll never have pain or sorrow; it will all go away." I listened and followed, dreaming of the relief I'd find once the water carried me away.

I wouldn't feel anymore. No sorrow, no guilt, no shame, no pain. I had to take that next step, and then just one more step, and it would all end. One. Two. Three. There would be a peaceful silence under the water, the kind of silence you find in meditation or prayer. I needed to take that third step.

My foot floated up as I began to step into the void. I was calm and even hopeful. I looked up into the rain, and suddenly my son's face cut through the stormy haze. Joseph was fourteen at the time, but the face that peered at me was that of the small boy he had been. Then it morphed into his teenage face with large brown eyes looking out from behind shaggy bangs that strayed over his eyelids. I heard him yell, "No, Mom, no! I need you. Don't go!"

I was so startled that I fell back from the edge, fighting to keep my balance as the wind demanded that I move forward. I fell onto a patch of solid rock and then crawled back from the cliff, stunned as if I'd seen a ghost. I followed the path toward the front of the aging building, weaving between branches that clawed at me, demanding me to return. My salty tears mixed with the ocean water and with the droplets from the sky. Everything appeared as if I were underwater, blurry, moving, and disorienting. I felt dizzy. I hadn't yet grasped what had just happened.

I knew it was only a short walk from there to the house. I moved mechanically toward our cottage. Halfway there, I noticed a man approaching me. He was cloaked in rain gear, and the heavy rain made it difficult to see who it was. As I got closer, I heard a voice call to me. "Alicia, is that you? Are you okay?"

It was Jerry. He had gone out to look for me when I didn't return. Perhaps he had a premonition, or maybe it was simple concern. I don't know; I never asked.

"What are you doing out here? You have to go home. Let's get out of this storm." He took my arm and quickly led me back to the house. I allowed him to steer me back, and we returned in silence.

I dropped my clothes on the bathroom floor and turned on the shower. Standing in the hot water, I tried to wash away my tears and pain, but they kept coming in waves. I fell to my knees sobbing as the water washed over me, hot enough to steam the mirror but not hot enough to burn away the immense grief I had buried, which now washed over me. I don't know how long I was there. Eventually, I slipped into my pajamas and crawled into bed, hoping that sleep would overtake me so the silence of the unconscious might provide some relief.

The next day at breakfast, I told Jerry I wanted to go home although we had only been there a few days. I suggested that he and Joseph stay. He became angry and decided we should all go home. I never told him the truth about that night. I never told my son that he saved his mother's life with his love for me—our love for each other.

That night, I learned that love prevails even in the darkest moments. I captured this sentiment in a small locket I wore around my neck. Those words were later repeated during a shamanic ceremony at the top of a pyramid thousands of miles away.

Every change is a death and a rebirth. Every decision moves us toward one thing and away from something else. Yet we are unaware that each step creates the road we travel. So often, we don't fully understand the consequences of our choices, especially when we make decisions on a whim, without thinking through the future possibilities as we shift from where we were to where we are going.

After weeks at his brother's house, Napo returns to our apartment on the bay. Something has changed, but I can't define it. Every day, I feel like I'm paddling in a tidal race—a fast-flowing ocean current that forms irregular waves that are difficult and dangerous to navigate. The water churns, and once you enter it, there is no choice but to allow the kayak to move with the chaotic tides. Fighting means capsizing into violent ocean waters. I learned how to paddle in a tidal race by feeling the ocean and using my paddles for balance more than maneuvering. The irony is that to have any semblance of control and safety, you must release control over the churning water despite your fear.

Being with Napo is my personal tidal race. Sometimes his anger flares abruptly. Then, a few days later, he once again becomes the tender, wise man I love. I am never sure who will greet me when I awake. He begins to resent our community, as if he fears being discovered by those who care for me. Indeed, I have several conversations with my neighbors in which they question his motives and express concern for me. I brush it off and excuse his behavior, attributing it to the challenges he's had in adapting to American culture.

At Napo's insistence, we begin looking for another place to live. Our rent at the Compound is high, and I welcome the chance to find a place where I can reduce my costs. Traveling to and from Ecuador has grown expensive. In addition, I've been spending thousands of dollars on lawyers and fees for his green card application. At the same time, I begin to have difficulty booking clients. The energy that had filled my coaching practice is dissipating. I'm having difficulty closing business that had easily flown in before Napo came to the United States.

We find a one-bedroom ground-floor apartment in a nearby golf development and move in the fall of 2015. Being on the ground floor makes it easy to take Finn out or to watch him on the patio outside. It is a modern apartment, and we will save $600 a month while remaining in the same area, close to the bay, so I can take my kayak out from the Compound, where I left it under the watchful eyes of my neighbors.

"This is better," Napo remarks when he sees the apartment. "We can be private here. No one needs to know what we do, and I like the view of the woods." I am so happy with the modern conveniences and lower price tag that I fail to see how he is isolating me from people who have begun questioning his presence in my life. Alina and Steve, who lived directly below us at the old apartment, must have heard our arguments and noticed how aloof he was when we visited with them. However, I believe that everything will improve—a belief reinforced by the occasions when we all spend time together laughing and enjoying each other's company. In those moments, Napo engages with humor and charisma that belies his shadow nature.

Moving to the new apartment takes me one step further from my safety net and the people who can protect me. I am so in love with Napo—or perhaps entranced by the desire to dive deeper into my spiritual life with someone I consider a teacher—that I fail to see the consequences of moving away from my friends. Instead, I focus on a dream, an exciting possibility that closes my eyes to what lurks behind my choices. This move is one step closer to living in Ecuador. We remain at the new apartment for less than two years before we move entirely to his country—away from anyone who could shine light into the darkness that will eventually arrive.

— 15 —
AN OASIS IN ECUADOR

In January 2015, Napo and I conduct a women's retreat in Otavalo. We are both surprised at how well our work complements the other's. One night over dinner, Napo wonders, "What if we didn't use hotels for our retreats? What if we built our own place, used it for our retreats, and rented it out for others to host retreats?"

"Seriously?" I reply, looking up at him from my meal. "That never occurred to me. But where would we build it? It's too cold here in the Andes." The thought of living in the Andes full-time makes me shiver.

"I want to be on the coast. I have always wanted to live near the ocean since I lived in Guayaquil when I was young. Let's go to the coast, find land, and build a place for ourselves." He becomes animated, imagining what our lives will be like if we create what he calls "an oasis" for the soul.

"That's what we'll call it, Napo. We'll call it Quinta Oasis!" I exclaim as I catch his excitement. "Napo, I used to be in the hospitality business. If you can build it, I can run it. I know how to do that." And so, the plan is born. Another decision, another step on our journey together.

We visit the coast to begin searching for land. We reserve a room in Santa Marianita, a small fishing village a few miles southwest of Manta in the province of Manabí on the Ecuadorian coast. It is summer in the southern hemisphere, and we are not ready to return to the cold and snow of the Mid-Atlantic. From here, we begin our exploration, hoping to find a plot of land where we might build our dream.

I reserve a room at a beach hostel run by an older American woman who came to live in Ecuador over fifteen years ago. Linda is a character unto herself. "Brass balls" would be one way to describe this seventy-year-old woman. She is fearless and unapologetically speaks her mind. She also has a heart of gold and treats every guest as an old friend.

"Linda," I call from the terrace of our room. "Come join me for coffee."

She wears casual beachwear: knee-length khaki shorts, a short-sleeved blouse in a flowery print, and thick, comfortable sandals. Her purse hangs over her shoulder. She approaches, smiling and gesturing.

"Oh dear, I'm off to Manta for some shopping and to return a few things I decided I don't need." As she speaks, she rummages around in her purse. "I know I have the receipt here somewhere," she says once she reaches the terrace stairs. Her bag slips off her shoulder, spilling its contents on the tiles. I descend the stairs to help her and stop, shocked at the contents. On the ground, amidst lipstick, a wallet, tissues, coins, and torn pieces of paper, is a silver revolver with an ivory-like handle. Linda looks up to see my shocked expression. She picks up the pistol as calmly as if it were a tube of lipstick, smiles at me, then stuffs it back into her bag. "You never know when it might come in handy," she says with a look that tells me I am in on her secret.

The hostel guests are from the United States, Canada, France, and South Africa. As different as we are, we all enjoy drinking, eating, music, and dancing. There is a festive atmosphere. Linda generously takes the guests out to explore and introduces us to the market and restaurants in Manta, the large city nearby. The beach is at our door-step, a constant invitation to swim during the day and stroll during the evenings.

When Napo and I tell Linda about our dream of buying land, she introduces us to a guest who bought land an hour south of Manta in a fishing village called Puerto Cayo. Anna is Canadian and will be retiring soon from a long tenure as an executive in a Canadian corporation. She tells us she is an engineer, which becomes apparent when we see her detailed schematics. Laying architectural drawings on one of the picnic tables, she explains the layout and her vision for the home she plans to build.

"The plot is right on the beach. I always wanted to live on the beach," Anna shares. "And now I will. My husband will be joining me later."

"How did you find the land?" I ask, curious since we, too, are looking.

"I scouted areas in Manabí, contacted real estate people, and kept searching until I found Puerto Cayo and the plot. I envisioned living there, far enough from the city of Manta but close enough to access its services. The house will be a large two-bedroom with the kitchen, dining room, and living room as one open space in the center. That's where we'll spend most of our time. I'll also build a few guesthouses that I can rent later."

The next day, Linda drives us to Anna's land. It's larger than I imagined, and it's on the beach with a view of Isla de la Plata (Silver Island), a protected island off the coast that can only be explored with authorized nature guides. Anna walks the property, pointing out where she plans to build the house and other spaces.

I admire how well she has thought through her plans. She is confident, and her enthusiasm about living on the coast is contagious. Napo and I are determined to search for a plot that will eventually become our oasis. We meet with real estate agents for the next few days and visit properties and land for sale. But our enthusiasm wanes as one plot after another proves ill-suited for our vision.

"I'm not sure we'll find what we're looking for, Napo," I say one evening. We sit on our room's terrace with glasses of wine. "Everyone seems to want to sell at crazy prices, perhaps because they see me as a rich *gringa*."

"*No te preocupes, así es en Ecuador,*" he responds with a smirk— don't worry, that's how it is in Ecuador. "We will find our place. Tomorrow we will look at one last property near Puerto Lopez. I have spoken to the man, and he says he has land with an ocean view. He has the documentation that's required to sell. We will meet him at the bus station. For now, let's enjoy being here at the beach."

The next day, we take the bus to Puerto Lopez, a forty-five-minute ride on the coastal highway. We meet a short, scruffy man in oversize shorts, a torn T-shirt, and sandals that seem glued together. The odor of old whiskey floats around him. This does not inspire confidence. A taxi takes the three of us from the bus station to an overgrown plot overlooking the town. "Here we are," the man gleefully announces.

Looking west, Napo asks, "Where is the ocean view?" Despite the elevation, all we see are houses and trees. The only indication that the ocean lies beyond is its blue reflection on the clouds.

"It's over there," he says, pointing in the same direction. "But the trees and houses are in the way." Napo turns to look at me. The look on my face speaks the words I cannot utter.

Exasperated, I swear under my breath as I turn away. "What the fuck?"

Looking toward the back of the property, I notice a tall stone wall with markings I can't understand. "What is that wall?" I ask the man.

"Oh, that. That is the cemetery. Don't worry. Spirits cannot climb walls, and it will be quiet here for you."

I can't decide whether to laugh or cry. I walk away instead, leaving Napo to insult the man for wasting our time.

An hour later, we have coffee in Puerto Lopez. Napo goes to the restroom while I wait at the table. The waitress is friendly and asks about our stay. "We are looking for ocean-view property to build a home, but we haven't found anything we like."

Her eyes light up and she says, "I know someone who has a large property for sale, four thousand square meters with an ocean view. It is in Salango, five minutes south of here. I can call the owner now, and he can show it to you."

"Of course," I cynically respond just as Napo returns. She tells Napo about the property, and he decides we should see it.

"Napo, I'm tired of being lied to and tired of people wasting our time or trying to take advantage," I tell him between sips of coffee.

"What is one more place, Alicia? We are here, and it's close by. Let's look. But if you like it, you must act like you don't like it," he advises.

We take a taxi to meet the owner, Augustin, in Salango. He is shorter than I am, a muscular middle-aged man with skin darkened by the sun and a glint of malice in his eye. His clothes are dirty and mismatched. A gold chain hangs from his neck and drops into the tank top he wears under his shirt. I immediately sense a con. Napo does, too, but he plays along, masking his intentions with charisma.

Augustin begins his pitch. "I have been a farmer, but now I'm too old to farm and work in another city. I want to sell the property so I can move to Guayaquil. The land is untouched, with native trees for shade. And you can see to the ocean." We climb a steep hill as he rambles about life in this small village called Río Chico. He tells us his wife and children live in one of the homes nearby, and he volunteers to help us with construction. We climb a dirt path for about fifteen minutes. My optimism is stiffening as much as my legs. Finally, we reach the top and turn around.

There's a reason I don't play poker. Everything is written on my face. I turn to glimpse the setting sun, hanging low over the ocean's horizon between two tall hills. The sky glows orange, yellow, and purple. My breath catches in my throat at the beauty of the scene.

Napo glances at my face and winks, unseen by Augustin. I know he is thinking the same thing. This is it. This is the land we must buy.

His face is like stone, however. He pauses, picks up a small stem, and puts it in his mouth, chewing it deliberately before he comments, as Augustin anxiously awaits his response. "It's very nice, but it will need too much work," Napo says finally. "There is no water or electricity here. No road. This will be very expensive." He has begun to negotiate.

I return to the United States two weeks later. Napo stays behind to conclude the property transfer. The land is part of a *comuna*. In *comunas*, the community owns the land. The buyer purchases the rights to use the terrain through a document called *certificado de uso posesión*. The buyer pays the seller to transfer "the right to use," and the *comuna* charges a fee as well. I do not understand this when Napo asks me to send him the money for the deposit. I later discover that the only name on the certificate is his. He will not add my name to the document until I force him to do so years later. It is the first of many things that Napo hides from me over the years.

In March 2015, Napo begins construction with only a faint idea of what to build. I share my drawings and designs for him to use as he levels and tiers the land. He asks for more money, yet he ignores my requests to discuss the plan. Buildings slowly rise out of fallow land, and the vision of what will become Quinta Oasis starts to form. The name is symbolic of healing and hope in times when it seems that these qualities have forsaken us. Trusting Napo to supervise the construction, I continue managing my business and activities in the United States.

We spend hours on Skype almost every day, talking about construction progress without noticing that arguments and conversations about money have displaced our discussions about shamanism and spirituality. Napo shares his struggles to monitor workers who try to steal from him or shortcut necessary tasks.

"I need you to send me another ten thousand dollars this month," he demands during a Skype video call in May 2015, when we still live at the Compound. "I'm starting on the next house and must buy materials and hire additional labor."

"Napo, I'm not a bank," I reply, annoyed. "I can't keep withdrawing money from my retirement funds. I have to pay penalties and taxes, and my business is not doing well right now."

"I don't care!" he shouts. "I have already made commitments and must pay bills." My anger rises, yet I feel helpless to argue with him. A surge of guilt hits me, followed by intense anxiety. How will I afford to keep sending money? Why is he making commitments that require payments for things that should be planned well in advance?

"You need to pause the construction until I have more funds in the bank, Napo. I can't sustain this." My statement sounds more like a plea, and I realize I have already lost this fight.

"We must continue. There is no stopping, Alicia. We must be audacious to build the Oasis." His tone is firm. "Send me the money this week via Western Union," he demands.

Then, hearing shouting in the background, I ask, "What's going on there?"

"I need to go. The workers are calling me." And with that, the screen goes blank. I slump into the sofa cushions, resigned and disheartened. "Now what?" I ask myself. I walk to the kitchen and pour myself a glass of wine. Looking out to the Chesapeake Bay, I notice the afternoon light changing into the glow of early evening. Birds nestle into the giant oak tree's branches, singing the day's last notes. The bay is calm this evening, a glass pane reflecting the few billowy clouds in the sky. Despite the argument, a peaceful feeling washes over me. I take Finn and my wine and go out to the dock. The last remnants of the day fade, and the stars begin to peep out of the dark blue sky. "Now what?" I ask again. Tonight, the question is left unanswered, hanging in the breeze.

Over the months that follow, we travel back and forth between the United States and Ecuador. I love spending time in Ecuador, away from the busyness of my life. There, I am more attuned to the natural world. It makes me long for a more natural pace. The more I visit Ecuador, the more I miss it when I return to Maryland.

In May 2015, Napo receives his temporary resident card. Due to an immense government backlog, we won't obtain his final resident card until 2017. Napo travels on this provisional card but has limits on how much time he can spend out of the United States. As a result, we are often apart for months when he returns to Ecuador, if only for a short time. I frequently travel to meet him there, spending up to two months at a time living in Quito and exploring the country with him.

Napo stays in Ecuador until July 2015. When he returns, we continue the same routine we'd had when he first came to the United States. For the next few months, he works with clients at my office in Annapolis. During this time, I deepen my knowledge of shamanism by attending client sessions and witnessing the healing power that a true shaman can enlist. My respect for the shaman grows, as does his control over me. Being privy to the healing of individuals who are deeply wounded, some physically but most emotionally and spiritually, makes me question how I lead my life.

Before our first healing session, Napo coaches me to stay on the other side of the room, opposite from the client, and not respond to anything that happens. "Napo," I say, "what could possibly happen that would surprise me? You've taught me so much already."

He is arranging the altar and preparing the seating area, burning palo santo and sage to clear the space. We store the altar items in the middle of the room, in a cabinet draped with a brightly colored Ecuadorian runner. Napo chooses several small stone totem animals and carefully places them on top of the cabinet. Joining them are items from all four elements: air, water, earth, and fire. Then he arranges a flute, seashells, crystals, stones, and several candles on the runner with a small ocarina, a stone rattle, and feathered and jeweled branches. His dark bottle—the one with the mysterious mix of rose water, herbs, and flowers—stands on the cabinet, unwrapped from its embroidered velvet pouch.

"Alicia, teaching you with words is different than the experience of working with me in a session. Simply do what I tell you and stay calm; you may see things you have not seen before."

I hide my inner smirk, thinking my coaching work has prepared me for tears, anger, sadness, and grief, all elements of transforming negative energy into positive energy. "I'll do as you say, Napo. Just let me know when you need assistance."

Today the client is an older woman (I'll call her Jane) who was in a car accident five years ago. She has not been able to walk without crutches. Her brother died in the same accident, and Napo and I agree that this loss contributes to her inability to heal. Friends of mine referred her to us.

When Jane arrives, she shuffles in on her crutches, pain showing on her face as she climbs the stairs to my office. After serving her a glass of water and leading her to the recliner, we begin the session. For the first thirty minutes, I translate Napo's questions and her answers. He then lowers her chair, and I cover her with one of the Ecuadorian blankets I keep in the office. As Napo instructs, I tell her to breathe deeply and relax, noting that it isn't unusual for clients to fall asleep during a session. As Napo blows palo santo over her, she closes her eyes and he begins to drum. In a few minutes, her breath shifts, following the cadence of the drumbeat. I sit on the other side of the room, breathing deeply and observing Napo as he drums, chants, and circles her, moving from her head to her legs and feet. The drumming lasts forty-five minutes, and it's clear that she is asleep or in a trance-like state.

I feel the air in the room on my skin. Puffs of smoke waft around Jane as if they have a life of their own. The sweetness of the wood enters my nostrils and flows into my lungs, relaxing my body.

Napo continues to dance around her with the rattle, then stops at her head, puts down the rattle, and holds her head between his hands. Her body stiffens, and her legs extend beyond the chair. Slowly, she begins to rise. I think I'm imagining it, believing that the blanket has shifted. But I'm wrong. She has levitated, opening a space between her body and the chair. I hear a sound like an animal crying, and her body begins to tremble.

Napo's glance reminds me of his instructions to stay calm. My chest feels like it will explode. I hold my breath. Trying to calm my mind, I recover my breath to relax. Jane's crying continues for about five minutes, and slowly her body returns to the chair. Napo opens the bottle with the sweet-smelling liquid, pours a bit into his mouth, then sprays it over her, the droplets imbuing the air with sweetness. He then adjusts the blanket around her as he looks at me with an intense gaze that holds me still.

After a few minutes of quiet, he approaches me and whispers, "Wake her up now, gently." I walk across the room and lightly tap her; speaking in a low tone, I invite her to awaken.

As she begins to move, I raise the recliner into a seated position. Jane's eyes are glassy, and she looks around the room as if searching for something she has lost. She finally says, "I feel like I've been asleep a very long time."

Jane is surprised she can stand without putting weight on the crutches. I translate Napo's instructions for her care, and we make another appointment for the following week. Each week, something similar happens. After five weeks, she returns with the news that she has been walking well enough to play eight holes of golf. She no longer uses crutches. She is delighted and thankful. We do not see her after that.

Once we are alone in the office, Napo blows palo santo over me and chants, removing any vestiges of negative energy that may have intruded into my energetic field. "Were you surprised, Alicia?" he asks seriously.

"Well, I can honestly say I have not experienced a healing session like this with anyone, but I suppose you're not anyone, are you, Napo?"

He smiles at the compliment. "You did well. Thank you. Now I'm hungry! Let's get dinner."

– 16 –
ENDINGS ARE BEGINNINGS

I love the stillness of evenings on the Ecuadorian coast. The birds meet the dusk with lullabies sweetened by ocean droplets hovering in the air. Like a prism, the light reflects the colors of the sunset, painting the property's buildings in orange, gold, and purple hues. The entire natural world rests between the hills that frame the setting sun as if Mother Earth's children are lying between her breasts. Tonight, an evening in late March 2017, I stand alone on the balcony of our house, reflecting on the journey that has taken me to this land at the equator, a place previously unknown to me but that I now call home.

Napo is in the United States while I remain on the property, which is still unfinished after two years. His resident permit requires him to spend months in the States; if he doesn't, he will lose his green card. I will return in April to pack and prepare for my permanent move to Ecuador in May.

The first time I stay alone at the property, Napo asks a neighbor and her husband to sleep in the house with me. I don't understand why. I will learn of the dangers a lone woman might encounter on a rural property only after making the permanent move. Then I'll realize my dogs and the pistol in my drawer will be inadequate if someone tries to harm me. But for now, ignorance is bliss, allowing me to savor the land's beauty and immerse myself in gardening, painting murals, managing the workers, and occasionally hosting a few guests.

This evening, I am content to watch the sunset with my dogs by my side, sipping a glass of chilled wine and dining on fresh shrimp and avocado. All struggle dissipates like the light that transforms into darkness, leaving me with the scent of palo santo trees and the echoes of the night birds.

The years after purchasing the land have been chaotic—we've been traveling between countries, spending months apart and months together, balancing two different lives and cultures. I've tried to resurrect my business online, knowing the shifts in my living situation drain my energy. However, my focus now lies on Ecuador, which shows in my business dealings.

My visits to Ecuador portend the difficulties I will face living in the *comuna*. The Ecuadorian workers are unreliable and, at times, thieves, stealing building supplies in the middle of the night and doing as little work as possible. Our neighbors resent us, believing a wealthy American has come to take over their community. To maintain good relations, we donate food to the elderly and supplies to the local school. When asked if we will donate the front portion of our land to make a roundabout on our dead-end street, we do so without hesitation. But regardless of what we do to support the community, they make it clear we are outsiders.

In May 2017, I sell most of what I own in the United States and prepare to move to Ecuador. Each item I touch means making decisions about the past or the future. Each item is tangible evidence of a memory, and I have to decide whether to keep the object or release it, only to have it remain in the recesses of my mind.

Alone in my mostly empty apartment, I am confronted by the reality of my move. In the week before I leave, I have two visitations, spirits that toy with me. I am first visited about seven days before my departure. I've already left Finn with Jerry and Joseph so I can pack without upsetting him. I'm alone in the apartment.

After a morning of choosing what to keep, what to give away, and what to store, I am physically and emotionally exhausted. I crawl into my bed and draw the covers over me. Between sleeping and waking, there is a lull where we drift in semi-consciousness. Here, the veil that separates us from the metaphysical world is lifted. I'm aware that I am in bed and not quite awake. My eyes are closed.

I lie on my side with the sheet over my head to keep out the light when I feel the mattress shift as if someone has sat down beside me. I quickly become present but do not open my eyes. My chest tightens as I feel a weight on my body, pressing me into the bed. I want to call out, but my voice eludes me. I try to move but am paralyzed. I don't dare open my eyes. At the same time, I begin to hear a chorus of voices, a million voices all at once, singing and chanting. The encounter feels both singular and collective, as if there is one entity made of millions of energies. The voices seem to lift in prayer, and despite my fear, I am enthralled by the chorus. I don't know how long this event lasts. Slowly, the voices recede and the weight lifts from my body.

Frightened, I call Napo in Ecuador. He interprets the event as ominous, dark spirits attempting to frighten me out of moving to Ecuador. He tells me to yell at them to go away, saying I will likely be visited again.

"But they didn't feel dark, Napo," I explain. "It was as if many spirits were praying for me, healing me. Just the opposite of what you are saying."

"You do not know of these things, Alicia," he responds, annoyed at my alternative interpretation. "You are with a shaman. Remember that. You will experience things in the metaphysical world, spirits attempting to hurt me through you. Do as I say, and you will be safe."

Years later, I will realize the chorus was a song of protection. The spirits were sent by the three shamans I had encountered in my dream years ago. They were indeed praying for me, knowing I was stepping onto a path where I would dance between light and dark, liminal spaces I had walked in forgotten lifetimes.

The following day, I stay in bed after waking, cuddled in my blankets until I feel a tug. Someone, or something, pulls on the blanket at the foot of the bed. I sit up and grab the blanket in a tug-of-war with an unseen energy.

The room looks as if it's underwater, everything wavy and moving. I can see the large closet door melting and then solidifying. I hold tight to the blanket, sensing that the spirit is teasing me but means no harm. Slowly, the room comes into focus as the tugging ceases.

This time, I call Carlos. He explains a concept the shamans call plasma, a kind of magnetic field. I had experienced the plasma state, allowing me to interact with the spirit or spirits that had come that morning.

"They know you are leaving your life here, Alicia. They want you to stay, but you must go. Tell them to go away and leave you alone," Carlos admonishes, reinforcing what Napo told me yesterday.

A few days later, I leave the United States to begin my new life in Ecuador. I cannot imagine how intertwined my life will become with the metaphysical world of shamanism.

On May 30, 2017, I arrive in Ecuador with ten Sterlite boxes filled with household items we need for the retreat center. My few remaining things have been packed and put in storage or boxed and shipped to Ecuador.

We spend the night in Quito before leaving for the coast the following day. It is a ten-hour drive from Quito to our property in Salango. I sleep most of the way, waking for short stops. When we arrive, the workers meet us and carry the boxes to our house.

That evening, Napo proudly walks me around the property. "This is our oasis, Alicia. This is where we will live and work and heal others. But first, we must never forget that we are spiritual beings." He pauses.

"*Bienvenida a su nueva vida*, Alicia." Welcome to your new life. He embraces me for a long time, welcoming me to the life that will change me forever.

In June, the mornings start off cloudy. Here, in the southern hemisphere, winter begins in June and lasts through November. I've never seen rain pour from the clouds with such intensity. A cleft in the soil between two buildings turns into a ravine with muddy water rushing from the upper level, over the road, and down to the garden level like a multi-tiered waterfall. Something else we must fix to avoid washing out the road.

The valley between our property and the ocean is painted in a palette of green. Everything smells fresh in the morning. I stand on the balcony, wrapped in my robe, drinking a strong cup of coffee. Napo enters the house followed by our dogs, Chief, Bella, and Lula. They leave a trail of muddy footprints.

"*Buenos días*, Panterita," Napo greets me. "What is for breakfast?"

Every morning, Napo wakes up at four o'clock. He spends the first two hours of his day in contemplation, drinking his two cups of green tea. I peer out of the bedroom to watch him sit on the sofa, looking out the balcony door as the sun rises, reflecting its light from behind our house onto the garden below. I won't rise until eight in the morning, enjoying a few moments in bed by myself. If I delay, Napo will open the bedroom door and allow the dogs to rush in, jumping on top of me with a fervor born of my closeness to these animals.

This morning, he has been outside greeting workers and assigning the day's tasks. He is in a good mood and is happy with the progress being made. "Two eggs and toast?" I ask, anticipating the answer.

"*Sí, como siempre.*" He smiles, noticing the eggs boiling on the stove. "Today, I will go into town for more supplies. Would you like to come?"

"Yes. Let's do that and get lunch while we're in Puerto Lopez," I suggest.

"Good idea. Maybe a walk on the beach after lunch to see if we spot any humpback whales? Yes?"

"Perfect," I respond, hoping to glimpse these magnificent creatures breaching the surface.

Between June and October, humpback whales migrate to the Ecuadorian coast to give birth in its warm waters. By August, you can spot the new whales swimming alongside their mothers. I never tire of seeing them jump high above the waves in delight. Whenever I go snorkeling, the awe and wonder I feel at sharing the ocean's depths with these creatures inspires me to write and fills me with gratitude for my life here.

By ten in the morning, we are in a taxi heading into Puerto Lopez, only a ten-minute drive from the property. The town is bustling with activity. You can always identify the tourists. The knee-length khaki shorts, straw hats, sneakers, and camera are dead giveaways. In contrast, the locals look sloppy in dirty sandals, printed shorts, and torn mismatched tank tops that are too tight around their protruding bellies. This is a town of haves and have-nots, primarily have-nots. It's a fisherman's village whose main street is dotted with restaurants, tourist shops filled with knickknacks, and bars illuminated with neon lights even in the daytime.

Napo and I greet the hardware shop owner while waiting in line to be attended to. The store is family owned and run. "*Hola*, Don Luna." The man behind the counter greets Napo warmly but formally. "What can I help you with?"

Napo pulls a folded sheet of paper from his pocket—a list of supplies. The shop owner takes the list and enters the vast room behind the counter. Its aisles are filled with hardware, tools, and building supplies. He begins pulling our goods from the shelves.

"One hundred twenty," he says to Napo, who turns to me, indicating I should pay. I remove the money from my purse and pay for the supplies. One of the clerks fills a cardboard box with our purchases.

"We will leave the box here while we have lunch," Napo tells the shop owner. It's not a request.

"*Sí, claro*," the owner replies. "Come after two when we return from lunch."

There is still mud in the streets from the previous night's rains. We navigate the puddles on our way to our favorite *hueca*, a hole-in-the-wall. The *huecas* offer the freshest traditional foods and are the cheapest restaurants. Tourists do not eat here, but locals like us provide a steady stream of customers. Most of the town knows us by now, and we are greeted as regulars.

Fried fish, plantains, and beans are on today's menu. We order freshly made lemonade as our beverage. We sit at a table with other locals. The waiter recognizes us and, with a smile, delivers our meals. Napo and I talk about the property as we eat. Soon we are ready for the bill, a mere three dollars each.

"Let's go to the beach for our walk," I suggest. We stroll a few blocks from the restaurant to the beach and walk for about thirty minutes. Boats filled with tourists eager to see the whales appear as dots in the ocean. I'm grateful Napo reminded me to bring a hat, as the sun makes my skin tingle.

We stop to dip our feet into the ocean. The water is cool and refreshing, a contrast to the hot sand we have been walking on. Small ripples surround our feet as we playfully kick water at each other. We keep walking through the water until we reach the boardwalk. We sit to put on our sandals, then return to the hardware store and take a taxi home with our purchases.

"That was a nice afternoon, Napo," I say as we unload supplies on the upper terrace.

He smiles. "*Sí*, Panterita. *Hay que disfrutar también*." We must also enjoy ourselves. The day ends with our ritual of drinking wine and watching the sun set over the ocean, each of us quietly in our own world, dreaming of what is possible.

— 17 —
THE SPIDER DREAM

Time flows like a river. Sometimes it is robust and rapid, and other times the current slows so much you forget there is movement. Time becomes a limiting concept in a life that no longer recognizes the artificial boundaries of time and space. There is no anchoring as the river changes its pace and flow. You learn to swim with the tide or drown against it.

A month after I move to Ecuador, an urgent phone call from my sister takes me back to the United States. My mother is dying.

I'm cleaning the kitchen after breakfast one morning in late June when my cell phone rings. When I see my sister's phone number, I know this will not be good news.

"Alicia," she says, "Mina has taken a turn for the worse. She is barely conscious. They are saying that she may not live much longer. You have to come home right now."

I suppress the fear in my gut and block tears as I ask what happened. My mother was diagnosed with dementia almost ten years ago. After caring for her at home, we finally moved her to a facility. We hated ourselves for doing this, but there was no choice. Now her body has finally begun to fail, shutting down bit by bit. She has decided to leave a life marked by suffering, loss, and pain.

I adore my mother. Before Alzheimer's, she was always my best friend, the one person who would love me unconditionally, even if she disagreed with my decisions or behavior. I love both of my parents, but my father died during my sophomore year in college. He missed most of my adult life. My mother beamed at my college graduation, knowing the sacrifices we had made so I could get the education my parents felt I needed to succeed. The day I graduated, Mina gave me a special gift. Sitting on my bed in my dorm room, she passed me a small box.

"This is for you, *hija*. It signifies my love and appreciation for you," she said as she handed me a small white box tied with a delicate pink ribbon. I sat beside her as I opened the box, revealing a gold ring of two intertwined hearts. I cried as I hugged her. I always felt we had been connected regardless of distance. She also recognized this.

Now, I twirl the same small ring on my finger as I tell Napo about my sister's phone call. "I have to go right now. My mother is dying," I repeat.

"How will you go?" he asks. "We don't have money for a flight."

"We do for this one," I answer, surprised and annoyed that his first consideration is the expense. "I'm going," I say firmly.

When I arrive, I sit with my mother and chant to her. I beg her forgiveness for the stupid things I did to hurt her and, with great love, speak my permission for her to go on her final journey. She dies the day after I arrive. Yet, as I will later discover, Mina continues to protect me. Her voice will save me months later, when violence enters my home in Ecuador.

Every day I find some time to be alone. I record the events of my life in my journal. So many seem insignificant—small rituals that keep me grounded. I spend my days pruning the fruit trees, harvesting the maracuya to make juice and cookies, learning to make empanadas the way my mother used to, and going for long walks to sit by the ocean and listen to her teachings. These simple routines allow me to shift into a spiritual life with a shaman whose teachings settle into my body, mind, and soul.

I no longer seek work in the business world and only take work that comes from referrals or past clients. The work that enlivened me in the past now feels out of place, incoherent in a life devoted to the land, the community, and my spiritual development. Like a musical note that is out of tune, the language of the world begins sounding foreign to me. I have now lived in Ecuador full-time for a year. It is hard to imagine returning to my previous life. I am transforming, but I have no idea how much until I dream of the spider.

Throughout my life, dreams have been significant. They're messages I don't always understand—at least not until much later—and they open the portal to other forms of knowing. This extrasensory antenna has been with me from the beginning, an inheritance of a culture that is much closer to the spiritual than the culture into which I was born.

I know I am going through a transformative process the likes of which I have not previously known. My dreams are prophetic, intense, and so vivid that I often wonder where my spirit has traveled during the night. These dreams feel like journeys undertaken when the soul is drawn to explore unknown realms, an intrepid adventurer returning with a new sensory perception and wisdom that appears with the sunrise, like a sudden and enlightened knowing.

I don't remember falling asleep, but I do remember walking. The trees tower over me and the land is moist, the way it is between summer and fall. It is late afternoon and the sun drops in the west, creating shadows that dance like wood nymphs and tree fairies accompanying me on this shamanic journey. This place feels familiar; the woods smell of musky sweetness and the path rises and falls, down and around, reminding me of the woods behind my apartment on the Chesapeake Bay.

I know where I am going. Something, someone, is waiting for me. This appointment has been made elsewhere, but I am here to keep it.

At the end of the path, a tall, beautiful woman dressed like an Amazon, severe and unflinching, guards the entrance to a gaping hole on the side of the mountain. She motions for me to enter, more like a command than an invitation.

My eyes slowly adjust to the darkness. I reach for a torch that has been conveniently inserted into a crevice in the wall—an invitation to go deeper. The flame is dim. Shadows flicker against the cold stone, making me believe I am not alone.

My breath is shallow in my tightening chest. My hands, wrapped around the wooden stick, are sweating, not from heat but from a fear that vibrates in all the cells in my body. The low tunnel shifts and swerves like a deserted roller coaster track, going up and down until, finally, I enter a giant cavern that seems to be at least six stories high.

The ground is covered in sticky moss that grows along a small lagoon of dark water, its edges lined with glistening stones of all shapes and sizes. Somehow, light reflects on the surface from higher reaches yet unseen.

The sounds of water dripping down the walls and the loud echoes of my heartbeat are interrupted by a slight rustling in the darkest recess. It grows louder. Something is approaching.

A gargantuan spider emerges from the shadows, much like an oversized tarantula, imposing and frightening, almost as tall as the cavern itself. It slowly lumbers toward me, drool slipping through its fangs, its green eyes flashing, approaching me as I stand paralyzed. I feel like a small David holding a toy spear before this Goliath. The giant spider advances until it towers over me, yet I do not move. I think I will die at any moment, but my stubborn streak refuses to back down.

I stand motionless, and a strange and overwhelming calm overtakes me. I'm not sure if it is resignation, surrender, or the sudden awareness that I'm the one who made this appointment. I volunteered for this. And she is simply here keeping her end of the deal.

And so begins our wordless conversation, silently transmitted between us.

Me: Why have you come?

Spider: I'm here to protect you.

Me: Protect me from what?

Spider: To protect you from the material world.

Me: Are you going to kill me?

Spider: If your death is necessary to protect you, I will kill you.

Me: How will I learn to protect myself?

Spider: Be wise. Honor your wisdom.

Me: How will I recognize my wisdom?

Spider: Listen to your heart. Trust your feelings. See with the eyes of spirit.

Me: How will I know?

Spider: You will feel peace.

Me: What will happen when I feel peace?

Spider: You will no longer need anything that does not serve you. All obstacles will be removed. Anything that holds you back will be released.

Me: Where am I going?

Spider: You are going home.

Me: Will you kill me?

Spider: No.

Me: Will you stay here or come with me?

Spider: I will be watching you from the shadows.

Me: Are you a friend?

Spider: No.

Me: Are you an enemy?

Spider: No.

Me: Who are you?

Spider: I am you.

Me: Can I choose?

Spider: Yes.

Me: I choose love.

Spider: That is good.

Me: Why is that good?

Spider: Because love conquers all. Love is power.

Me: I am love.

Spider: Yes, you are.

Me: I am free.

Spider: Yes, you are.

Me: I am whole.

Spider: Yes, you are.

Me: I am wise.

Spider: Not yet, but you are on the right path.

Me: I want to cross the river.

Spider: You will.

Me: How?

Spider: With faith, with love, with wisdom, with consciousness, and with suffering.

Me: Must I suffer?

Spider: Yes, it is part of the process.

Me: I'm afraid.

Spider: Do not be afraid. You are more powerful than you know. Now you will reenter the world.

The spider bows down, and in one quick motion, her fangs cut my body in half, then slice again and again until all that is left are bits of bone and rivers of blood. At that moment, I become awareness, a simple energy witnessing the evisceration of a body I once occupied. I am not afraid—I'm curious and detached as I watch myself disappear along with all I thought I was.

She spins a cocoon of sticky silver threads, into which she places all my pieces. She dips the bundle into the lagoon's dark waters over and over again. Then she carries the dripping bundle to a stone table. It looks like a baby swaddled tightly in a blanket, only without a head.

Two women appear dressed in long white robes. They carefully unwrap the bundle and methodically arrange the pieces of my being, chanting sacred music in an unknown language that echoes throughout the chamber as the spider observes.

Piece by piece, my body begins to reappear. I am not in the body; I'm an energy floating nearby, observing their task like a customer waiting for the tailor to complete the suit I will wear back into the world.

The spider gradually withdraws into the shadows as my energy merges with the body on the table. The women dress me in a plain white cloth robe similar to their own. I humbly bow to them and receive the torch one of them hands me.

I walk back through the tunnel, imbued with a warm sensation and a peaceful feeling that the appointment has gone well. Once I emerge from the cave, I return the torch to the Amazonian woman . . . and wake up.

A new day, a new life, has begun.

* *

The spider dream confirms that I am in the process of transforming. Still, I do not recognize how much I have surrendered my power and agency to Napo. A strange dynamic is at play between his feminine energy and my masculine energy; however, it will be years before I recognize that our trouble stems from corruption in the integration of these two facets.

Napo has difficulty integrating his feminine side. He names the woman within Cora. We choose to name my masculine energy George. When Cora arises, she takes over his body, literally. His musculature softens, and he physically transforms into a more feminine version of himself. During those days, he removes himself from the world to protect Cora. George is the balancing energy on those days, so I manage the workers and take over the day-to-day operations. I repeatedly deny my own feminine side to balance Napo's feminine energy, survive the struggles of building the Oasis, and—later on—be strong enough to fight for myself.

The spider dream portends that to reclaim my life, I must reintegrate the feminine and masculine as part of my spiritual rebirth. My path forward is a shamanic journey, a descent into my night of the soul to deconstruct and restructure my life. I need to reclaim the discarded parts of myself that split during my original separation from spirit at birth—the parts I have ignored, devalued, and repressed in my quest for success in the material world. My dismemberment dream is the initiation into a shamanic process of renewal that will bring me closer to my desire to integrate the secular and the sacred. My spiritual battle will be to reclaim my connection with the sacred feminine so I can understand who I am as a conscious, integral being.

On the one hand, Napo encourages me to become that spiritual warrior; on the other, he strikes her down when he feels threatened. Through his teachings and my intuition, I understand that the element at the core of my lifelong quest, and the path to return to my connection with the divine, is the shamanic concept of *el sentimiento universal* (universal love) and *amor propio* (self-love). But I will have to fight for it and suffer, just as the spider has warned me.

Shamanism speaks to our divinity as particles of the Creator born of universal love. Connecting with that divine element establishes our existence as conscious beings and as representations of the Creator. The more we resist integrating our identity as spiritual beings, the more we suffer.

The process of individuation, or coming to wholeness, is an innate process that happens in all of nature. It's a process of becoming whole. Shamanism teaches the fundamental principle of acknowledging and surpassing what shamans call *la unidad* (the singularity) to reunite with *la totalidad* (the totality of all that is).

The lack of this understanding leaves us with our erroneous human view of the universe as an incoherent space/time field populated by unrelated bodies of matter that randomly exist in a pool of non-holistic relations. We lose the jewel of interconnectedness to the universe, its elements, and all living beings. We are multidimensional beings who are interdependent and integral to all life. Shamanism's cosmovision teaches that we are created from universal love from soul to embodiment to collectively express the creative divine powers of the living universe.

We are, indeed, so much more than our minds allow us to recognize.

— 18 —
MEETING THE SHAMAN WITHIN

There is no grace in the face of a shaman. It is raw, primitive, intense, tragic, and dark. And it is glorious, beautiful, expansive, and full of awe. Before I met Carlos, shamanism was a word I had seen on spiritual development websites and sites that combined a plethora of symbols, archetypes, and imagery of light and dark for more emphasis and mystery. Before I met Napo, I had read about shamans and had even spent six years apprenticing with his brother, yet, as I was to find out, I was more of a novice than I could've imagined. I look back on that naivete and ask, what was I thinking? No one in their right mind would develop a relationship with a shaman whose spirit is embodied here on earth but who experiences life in multiple realities. But reason had nothing to do with it. I only know what I felt when I first saw him and what I feel now, years later.

For better or worse, there I was, and here I am, writing a story that has gestated in me for years. It's a story I must write. Maybe in writing it, I will find that the past years have changed me more than I believe. Perhaps I'll realize that the summit of Ecuador's Chimborazo volcano is no higher than a spirit's potential to evolve in this lifetime. And maybe, just maybe, I will come to integrate the power of love, love beyond anything imaginable on this earth. If there is one thing I have learned, it is that love is not what I thought it was. It is so much more. And so am I.

* *

It's a sweltering hot day, the kind where you no longer distinguish between beads of sweat and the salty tears in your eyes. The workers labor under the hot sun for hours. First, they place columns of rebar into the foundation, rising toward the sky. Then they turn wooden planks into box-shaped molds that surround the rebar. After that, they pour bucket after bucket of wet cement into the columns. Tomorrow, the workers will remove the molds to reveal a set of concrete columns that will support a new house. Finally, we'll see some results.

I watch them work, covered from head to foot with old shirts and hoods, mixing cement, cutting rebar, positioning the wooden planks. They do these tasks repeatedly with occasional breaks for water and food. I wonder how hot they must be under all those clothes and the relentless equatorial sun. Such an irony that the sun brings tourists to the coast to bask in idleness, a stark contrast to the Ecuadorians who labor under it.

The workers stop at four o'clock, as if an internal alarm has gone off. They quickly gather their tools and personal items and, with their heads lowered, say brief goodbyes as they return to their homes. They have been here since seven o'clock, starting early due to the heat, and took only a short lunch break. I know that every dime I pay them will feed their families, women and children I've met. They've treated us respectfully and, in some cases, fearfully. It's important that this dream is not only for Napo and me but also for sustaining the community we now call home.

I quietly watch them from a lone chair in the only shady spot on the upper terrace. *I must be an odd creature to them*, I think. Women in this culture are more subservient—or appear to be—yet it is clear that women hold quiet power in each family. But I've always known: don't mess with the *abuelas*, the grandmothers. On their best days, they are wise and savvy, and on their worst days, manipulative and vengeful. Best to keep on their good side.

Napo and I make it a daily ritual to enjoy a glass of wine as we watch the sun set between the two mountains that frame the ocean. The view from our balcony is spectacular. During the southern hemisphere's summer months, the sunsets glow in deep hues of red, purple, orange, and yellow, like a painter gone mad with his paintbrush.

We sit quietly one evening, drinking in the breeze that cools the air as day turns to evening. I start making dinner with chicken, rice, and plantains, which are staples in our kitchen. After eating dinner and washing the dishes, I go to rest in the bedroom. But Napo calls me back. I sense what he wants and take my iPhone to record our conversation. And so, another lesson begins.

"I want to teach you about memory," Napo says. "Not the memory you think with your brain, but spiritual memory. With memory, everything repeats, and when consciousness awakens, you become aware of that repetition, and it is recorded."

He continues, "With body memory, we remember the past. When you are touched a certain way, you respond based on the past and the memory of a similar touch. Muscle memory reinitiates the same movement from before, even if that part of your body has not been active for a while. If the body fails, the memory of this failure stays and alters the muscle."

Napo explains, "Our genes retain memories of our ancestors, our parents, and their parents. These memories are inscribed in your DNA, reproducing something from an ancestor that has been before. If the person has trauma, then this memory is affected."

As I sit on the sofa, I feel myself being lulled into a trance by his voice. He uses this cadence with his clients during healing sessions. It is a rhythmic way of speaking; intonations rise and fall like musical notes, and the pauses between those notes create a momentary silence that in itself is healing. When we have these conversations, he instructs me not to use my mind to understand—he tells me to sense the concepts instead. This light trance state allows that shamanic wisdom to penetrate my subconscious, bypassing my mind and creating a subtle understanding that doesn't threaten the rational brain.

"We are the Creator's children because of that spiritual heritage through consciousness," he says. "When these memories are not integrated, the human has dementia and no spiritual memory. He only understands himself as a biological being, nothing else."

Napo has been sitting in a chair across from me, leaning his forearms on his legs. He stretches and stands, then walks to the balcony doors, looking out over the property as he continues his lesson.

"The planet has consciousness even though the human does not. Because of a derailment called evolution, the human being loses this reality to reinforce the other reality, the one of the material world."

He had shared this knowledge with me in Peguche when I first met him. Today, the lesson is amplified. Through my connection with him, I understand this teaching at another level. Now it is time to learn how to apply it.

He continues, turning to look at me, "Remember that you are from spirit. Consciousness is the memory of spirit, but I want you to apply that to the mind's or body's memory of the collective so you can teach others without them knowing it—they cannot understand it directly. They will intellectualize it if you tell them directly. Instead, hide it in something they can take in through the mind to connect to the spirit inside themselves. Provide subliminal messages of consciousness so that mind, body, and spirit combine—a trinity. This is how you will help people to integrate mind, body, and spirit."

I think of my storytelling as he explains how to help people expand their level of consciousness. Storytelling and metaphor are my art and my tools for enlisting my clients' imaginations. This helps them connect more deeply to the hidden parts of themselves, both light and shadow, that limit them to their beliefs and assumptions of how life should be.

"Humanity has spiritual Alzheimer's," Napo declares. "It has no memory of the God origin. No connection with spirit. You must recover your memory to help others recover theirs. You access it inside where the spiritual warrior is, in the unconscious, the dreams, and the shadows. Go in there to heal yourself. You suffer when you try to put the mind and body memory before the spiritual memory. Consciousness is superior to mind and body and punishes them."

His words remind me of my birth memory of floating in the universal womb, home to my soul, where my longing for that spiritual connection began.

"This is simple to talk about, but you must practice it daily," he insists. "Strive to remember when you lose your connection. There are days when the body or mind dominates and other days when the spirit does. When the body dominates your metabolism, your limbic system takes over. Notice and redirect that energy."

He continues, "When dominated by mind, you get delusions of grandeur, paranoia, or confusion. But problem-solving and creativity can also arise because the mind is very active. When the spirit flows, you enter the language of the universe. There is a cosmos waiting for you to return to it, so don't believe that what is obvious and superficial here will help you in the world of the cosmos outside of the planet. It will not."

Returning home to the cosmos, to the place of my soul's origin, is something I've always been trying to do. Hearing him speak of it and counsel me to look beyond the rational mind and the material world resonates profoundly and reflects the journey I have been on for my entire life.

"The more we resist integrating our spiritual identity, the more we will suffer," Napo continues. "The memory of the body and mind has its limits. Humans are trying to elevate that on top of consciousness, and it doesn't work."

He says, "Our lack of spiritual memory leaves us with our errone-ous cosmic view of the universe as a limited field of space and time, each separate from the other, and all others, as if all lives are unrelated masses of matter randomly existing next to one another without any connection or interdependence. This misunderstanding is the root cause of all suffering on this planet. You are here to heal this. But first, you must remember your true identity and heal yourself."

He returns to the sofa and sits quietly, his eyes soft. He sees some-thing far away, not in this room—perhaps not even in this world. We are both quiet for a few minutes. Then, turning to me, he announces, "And now it's time for bed. You will have dreams."

We get ready for bed. Napo is under the mosquito netting and almost asleep when I pull it over my side of the bed. I quickly fall asleep and dream.

At about four o'clock in the morning, I wake from a dream but can't remember it. The room is unusually light, with slivers of a silver glow peeking through the shutters. I am wide-awake and can't get back to sleep. Grabbing my robe and sandals, I leave the bedroom and head outside.

The moon is full, surrounded by a halo of light. The glow is so intense it almost looks like daytime. My dogs wake up and follow me to the terrace area. I just want to bask in that heavenly light, feeling all the cosmic energy running through me like an electric current buzzing inside.

The night is alive with sound. The unseen frogs in the wet grasses dominate the symphony with their high-pitched singing. Somewhere in the distance, an owl screeches. I can almost hear the flutter of the moth's wings against the lamps that light the path and the buildings' walls.

The evening sounds fill me until I feel like my chest will burst open. I sit in the moonlight, breathing the night air, cool and moist now, relaxing my body into a meditative state. From that stillness, a question arises: "Who would you be if you could dance between the worlds?"

Is the moon speaking to me? Does she whisper this profound question? Again, I hear the question: "Who would you be if you could dance between the worlds?"

Napo's lesson begins to take form inside my heart. There is no thinking involved in my attempt to understand. The shamanic wisdom simply integrates through the moonbeams that enter my soul.

"Who would you be if you could dance between the worlds?" the moon asks again.

I whisper, "I would be me."

Portals to other dimensions lie unseen by the human eye. Myths allude to them; we experience them as vortexes, points of energy on Earth that carry a powerful magnetic charge. We sense their energy when we are close to them. Some of us perceive it more than others. Places like Stonehenge in the United Kingdom, Newgrange in Ireland, Sedona in the United States, and Cochasquí in Ecuador vibrate with magical energy. These are well-known locations, and researchers have documented these energetic portals.

Yet other spots are unknown to us, located in ordinary places, often intuited only by individuals who are sensitive to energy. The land where we built the Oasis was like this. I began feeling unusual energy on the property once I lived there. Napo and Carlos had already conducted ceremonies to clear the land of negative energy, but some remained. The area where we lived was home to the Manteño culture, a pre-Incan culture that occupied much of the Ecuadorian coast from 500–1531, lasting until the Spanish arrived around 1534. Manteños were respected for their navigational and fishing skills, and the fishing industry still flourishes today. They were great warriors and the first to fight against the Spanish. Like many ancient Ecuadorian cultures, this pre-Hispanic culture was polytheistic and considered the four elements of the sun, fire, water, and earth to be living energies. The shaman was the tribe's spiritual guide. He was the keeper of the wisdom traditions, and one of his responsibilities was communicating with spirits from the underworld on behalf of the community.

Perhaps it is no coincidence that I now live with a shaman on land that contains the same ancient vibration the Manteño ancestors had felt. While digging the foundation for our buildings, we find shards of pottery and fossilized shells, remnants of life on this hill. Behind the property is a circle of stones. I'll never know who placed it there, but I feel uneasy when I visit the area. Our two-story building is only fifty meters from that spot, behind a tall brick wall we built to separate our land from our neighbor's.

I discover the portal by mistake. We're completing the building and just painted the room on the ground floor, which will soon be home to an on-site caretaker. The door is open so the paint can dry in the breeze. I play with two of my dogs, Chief and Bella, in the outdoor kitchen nearby. When they run around the building, I don't think anything about it. Before nightfall, I close the door to the freshly painted room. When we call the dogs to dinner, only Lula and Bella come; Chief does not appear. I don't think much about it, though—he habitually runs away or hunts in the orchard.

When I call the dogs for breakfast, Chief is nowhere to be found. I begin to worry. "Napo," I say during breakfast, "I haven't seen Chief since we played on the terrace yesterday. I'm getting worried."

"Alicia, you know Chief hides sometimes. Perhaps he hunted and is hiding his prey? In any case, I'm sure he will appear soon." His tone is nonchalant.

Two days pass, and Chief is still missing. This afternoon, I start calling for him like I have since he disappeared. I'm on the outdoor terrace calling when I hear him bark. The sound comes from behind the building. Bella runs to the back, and I follow her. As I turn the corner, I hear barking from inside the caretaker's apartment, which had been empty when I was there earlier that day. I open the door and Chief runs out. He jumps up and I hug him. Curious, I enter the apartment. There is no sign that anyone, let alone a dog, has been in the apartment for several days. I call to Napo, who also heard Chief bark and is already walking toward me.

"Napo, I found Chief in the apartment," I say. "But I checked it this morning, and it was empty. So how could Chief appear in the apartment? No one has been on the property. How is this possible?" I speak so rapidly that I lose my breath.

Napo enters the apartment and stands in the middle of the room, closing his eyes. He remains there for about three minutes. Then, opening his eyes, he beckons me to stand with him. "There is a portal here, Alicia. Carlos and I missed it. Chief ventured through the portal. But he was able to return."

"What are you talking about? What portal? To where?" I ask anxiously.

"There are places everywhere that go unnoticed. They are doorways into other dimensions. Sometimes we get caught in these, but we forget. The mind cannot understand and refuses to remember. It is like a hole in the fabric of time and space. Shamans are familiar with these portals, and we seek them. You will sense a different energy if you close your eyes and still your mind. It may feel like the temperature in this spot is different. This property has several portals. But there is nothing to worry about."

He holds my hand as I close my eyes and shift my breath to an even rhythm. I notice a soft breeze caressing my skin and a lightness in the air around me. Soon, however, I begin to feel dizzy and open my eyes.

"That is enough," Napo says. "Tomorrow, I will do a cleansing here. But for now, let's feed the dogs and continue with our day. Tomorrow, I will teach you about the wisdom of the natural world and how to access our ancestral wisdom. It's time for you to understand this."

— 19 —
WISDOM KEEPER TO SHADOW MAN

During my years in Ecuador, I focus on my inner life and development. I continue my quest to merge the sacred and secular. My retreat center embodies that inquiry and becomes an offering to all who wish for a deeper dialogue with the mystery of their lives.

Many come after spending time with gurus, taking online help courses, working with coaches, and trying therapy—all without achieving what they want: the happiness and peace that comes from purpose and meaning-making. They come with their burning questions, seeking answers to secrets that cannot reveal themselves within the mindset of productivity, rushing, and winning.

I learn that nature is the ultimate teacher. I create weeklong experiences that intentionally interrupt guests' rhythms and disrupt their thinking. It takes days before my guests can connect to the earth, the water, and the animals. It takes days for the body and mind to relax so the soul can speak.

I take my guests to the ocean, offering them insights and asking questions that, like koans, bypass the ego mind and penetrate the unconscious, where the structures that formed their beliefs and assumptions lay hidden. I purposely make my guests groundless so they can recover their grounding within an environment they cannot control.

Their default answers to my questions work . . . until they don't.

New, more profound questions then surface, upsetting them. I teach my guests to live with grief, fear, and the limitations life imposes on them rather than remaining hostage to the illusions their egos create.

At the same time, I undergo my own alchemical process. Years of beliefs and assumptions melt away in a container that can no longer hold the expansiveness I face. Once I experience myself as something more than my mind has previously allowed, I can no longer return to my smallness. The tension between my desire to remain invisible and the soul's summons to scream to the world that I am here is painful. That is my actual work every day.

As construction difficulties challenge us, I fall prey to worry, anxiety, and helplessness, but in a different, unseen way. I feel responsible for building this property and pour my heart, soul, and savings into it, only to be battered and bruised by a steady outflow of expenses and criticisms. This causes more and more dissonance between what my soul asks and what I feel required to do.

Napo changes when I arrive to live full-time in Ecuador. He becomes angry and aggressive. He goes on rants, sometimes hours long, about existential karma and my failures as a spiritual being, mother, wife, friend, and businessperson. He ticks off all the boxes meant to tear me down.

He co-opts my quest and reflects my weaknesses instead of my strengths, giving me anger instead of love. I struggle more and more with my sense of self and lose myself in his darkness. I feel him absorbing me like a sponge absorbs water. I begin to disappear. I know it but feel powerless to leave. How can I leave behind an incomplete dream? How many people will I let down? Where will I do my work?

What if I'm a complete failure in my spiritual quest?

That's the most daunting question I ask myself.

The fighting and verbal abuse intensify in 2017, just months after my permanent move. One morning, Napo and I meet the carpenter who will build the large wooden gate at the property's main entrance.

He measures the door's dimensions, and then we move to the terrace to see the designs he's sketched on some sheets of paper.

"Señora, which one do you like?" the carpenter asks.

I motion to one with a curved top and a geometric design made of wood carvings.

Napo looks over my shoulder. "No, not that one," he says. "We want one that is simpler."

I know he is considering the cost, but I'm paying for it. "No," I say. "We need something that stands out. The gate is the first thing someone arriving at the property sees." I request that the carpenter give us an estimate and a more detailed sketch that's to scale.

After he leaves, Napo and I go into the house. I sense something is wrong, so I ask him about it. He explodes.

"How dare you contradict me in front of a worker! Don't you understand that you are undermining me? I need to be seen as powerful and in charge, and you, a woman, step in and put me down in front of the carpenter. Now he'll tell everyone, and they will disrespect me, judging me as a lackey to a woman."

"What? What are you talking about?" I ask incredulously. "He asked my opinion, and I gave it to him. And besides, I'm paying for it. It must be beautiful as they enter the property to make an impression. I'm not diminishing you. I'm working with you, not against you."

"That is not working with me. Here, the man is in charge. You are not in charge. You do not make decisions." His face flushes with anger.

What the hell? I think. *Where is this coming from?* Then I speak to Napo. I say, "Aren't you the one who said I had to be seen as strong and decisive? I had to command attention and not let anyone see me as weak. Aren't you the one who said I had an image to uphold as an owner of this property? How is that different than what I just did?"

Already I can see the double standard of machismo playing out. I did not expect it from him. Until now, I have never felt that either of us dominated the other. I've worked hard to express my desire for an equitable partnership. We've devoted many conversations to being life partners, to mutually supporting each other as we share our common purpose. Because of these discussions, our argument about the door takes me by surprise. I've missed the signs—I simply didn't want to see them.

My friend Sandy has tried to warn me. I love her like a sister, and we have been through so much together. Sandy is intuitive, and she senses Napo's darkness before I do. He knows it too. He convinces me she has kept me from growing. He also makes me believe she isn't a true friend; he says she has been manipulating me under the guise of friendship. He calls me foolish and naive. And I believe him instead of believing my longtime friend. When they say love is blind, this is what they mean. When it comes to Napo, I wear blinders and rose-colored glasses. I miss the red flags that others see.

He says, "You want to be nice. What is nice? Nice is when people take advantage of you. Nice is when you are a fool and allow others to manipulate you. You never think of malice, do you, Alicia? You only believe that people are good. They are not. Everything survives because one thing must dominate, be the predator, and the other thing must submit, be the prey. Only the ones that dominate have power and survive."

That's his philosophy. Something has to die or be subdued so something else can have power. It has never occurred to me that I will be the one who is subdued.

When we began our relationship, Napo and I spoke of metaphysical principles of the universal movement, the idea that all things are in constant motion and change. We also talked about how the initial memory that comes from the Creator is, at its source, pure love. He taught me about consciousness from a shamanic perspective, not the New Age framework.

In shamanism, consciousness is the memory of the Spirit. It is the initial memory. Napo calls it the gene of the Creator. The initial memory contains all that corresponds to the origin of the universe. We are the Creator's children due to that spiritual heritage through consciousness. Our spiritual process is to establish our existence as conscious beings, representations of the Creator, by connecting with the divine.

Where has that wisdom keeper, that shaman, that lover, gone? Like watching a magician playing a card trick, who first reveals what is visible only to be replaced with the unexpected hidden card, I have been fooled and don't realize it until too late.

We argue, and Napo storms out of the house when I won't back down. Chief has been standing outside the door, and when Napo leaves, he comes into the house and runs to me. I pour myself a glass of wine and sit on the balcony caressing Lula and Bella, who have also come to find me. These animals are my protectors, perhaps not physically, but they provide unconditional love that calms me when I feel unsafe.

I ruminate over what to do next and ask myself a question I learned years earlier: "What would love do?"

About thirty minutes later, Napo returns, now calmer. Silently, I pour him a glass of wine and hand it to him. "Napo, I want you to sit and listen to what I say. I do not want you to respond or talk until I am finished. Can you do that?"

This is not what he expects. Perhaps he expects a fight, more drama, or complete surrender; I don't know. He looks at me with questioning eyes and then says, "Yes, I will listen." He sits on the sofa with the wine I poured.

I speak from my heart but hold my ground. "One day, I asked you why you came to the United States. You said you came for me. That is not true. We actually don't know why, at least not yet. If we truly believe in the universe's wisdom, then life put us together for a reason—to learn from each other."

I pause and take a long sip of wine while I watch him. He leans forward for a moment, then rests back on the pillows and drinks a bit of his wine.

"You say you love me," I continue. "And you may, but you don't accept me. I do not think that is love. You say you love me from the essence of who I am, the particle born of the Creator, but you reject the human. When you do that, you make me a fragment, and I am not a fragment. I am whole. I do not deny my humanness nor my spirituality."

I continue speaking slowly and softly. "I love and accept all of you—the man, the spirit, and the shaman. That is why I stay. I want to understand all the facets that create your being, not only your person. I watch you navigate the material and metaphysical worlds, and I learn from you. I see my struggles reflected in your eyes, and I come to know you as a part of me." Napo is still.

I know the next part of the conversation will be difficult. I stand up from the sofa and go to the balcony door, gazing outside as if something out there might give me the courage to continue. Finally, I do. "You reject your human aspect, and because of that, you reject me. You reject the material world, and so you reject the world that formed me. You cannot see this because your shadow doesn't allow you to notice it. You speak to me of a unified wholeness, of the shamanic principle of *unidad* and *totalidad*, yet you deny that within yourself and do not live in alignment with your teaching. You split the world into what is acceptable and unacceptable to you, into lightness and density, and you pass judgment as if you are separate and superior. You miss that all of life, what and who we are, all that connects us to every living organism, is part of what makes us both human and spiritual."

I turn to look at him. "And so, I am left in your eyes as a disparate fragment of being because you cannot love my humanness with the same compassion as you love my soul. I cannot accept that. I will never allow anyone, not even you or another shaman, to tear me into pieces."

His chest lifts with a deep breath, but he does not move for several seconds. The sun throws its early evening rays into the room, lighting it with a golden color. Only the birds outside make any sounds. The dogs lie still and have not stirred. I stand at the balcony door, glass in hand, waiting for his reaction.

He finishes his wine, sets the glass on the table, stands without looking at me, and walks out of the house. I will not see him again until the following day.

When I wake up the next morning, Napo is having his tea. He looks up at me, smiles, and says, "*Buenos días*," as if nothing has occurred. I make my coffee and sit next to him at the table.

"Panterita, I want to say something, but very little. You dared to speak to me yesterday, and I noticed you have been integrating my teaching. I was quiet and will not speak beyond my comments now, but I will tell you why."

He pauses. "Language, words, are limiting. They quantify what cannot be defined. You cannot use the language of the world to express *el sentimiento universal*, the expression of the spirit. The language of consciousness is silence. Intuition is how we must develop wisdom, not thoughts or ideas constructed by the mind. How do you understand if you cannot use language? Through universal love, we can accept what is unknown and unknowable. Perhaps music, art, or nature can bring us into that understanding, but even those are from the material world and, therefore, can be quantified. Do not interpret my silence as anything more or less than universal love recognizing itself."

I don't respond. I don't know how to. I hope yesterday's short conversation helps him understand that I will stand my ground, but with love and compassion. His words float into my being as I close my mind to rationalizing their meaning. The following years will prove that the shaman may have understood, but the man did not.

– 20 –
BREAKING DOWN AND BREAKING OPEN

My first two years in Ecuador are broken up by occasional trips to the United States, sometimes for work but mostly to visit friends and family. I have changed since my move, and those closest to me notice during my visits. Darkness has entered me, keeping me at arm's length from them. I grow quiet or withdraw. Sometimes I simply show them what they want to see. But they know me well enough to see through these performances and worry that something is wrong. They know it before I know it.

My relationship with Napo suffers ups and downs. I attribute them to adjusting to a new culture and the stress of building the retreat center from the ground up. I feel myself changing, but I'm unaware of the undercurrent of those changes. I'm growing psychologically and spiritually, but I am slowly losing myself in other ways.

Before moving to Ecuador, I never swore—not because of some moral imperative but simply because those words had no place in my life. That changes once I move to Ecuador, where I eat struggle for breakfast. Every morning, I arm myself for battle. Some days, it's a battle with Napo. Some days, it's a battle with the workers. On my worst days, I battle myself.

"Shit" and "fuck" become my mantras.

The fucking pipe buried under the bathroom floor, which can only be changed by excavation and destruction, dares me to stay calm as water seeps onto the new pool tile.

The tarantula that jumps out from a pile of rocks to scare the shit out of me—*FUCK!*

The shitty man that pushes me verbally and physically, gaslighting me into feeling small and insignificant—*Fuck you!*

Fuck. Fuck. Shit. Fuck.

It feels so good to swear. Like a giant dam with a small crack that breaks open because it can no longer hold back the weight of the water, the words gush from my mouth, so fluid, so naturally.

I wonder why I was holding back before. At first, swearing feels dangerous, like the time in high school when I smoked my first marijuana joint in the woods with the bad boy of Newton, pretending to be cool but trying not to vomit.

Almost overnight, I become best friends with foul language. It isn't that I turn into a foul-mouthed delinquent. Swearing simply happens at the most appropriate moments, when I detach from caring about a situation because I care too much. There are plenty of those moments.

The irony is that many of my clients and followers view me as a deeply spiritual person who has it all together. We believe that spiritual people are unflappable, can see beyond distressing situations, and rise above them through a higher level of consciousness. In my work, I represent the calm in the storm for my clients. Some even say I am wise and spiritual. Yet there are days when I feel like an imposter putting on my imaginary white robes, doing my work, then returning to the forever-sweaty person whose deepest wish is not spiritual. I simply want to be clean for twenty-four hours.

Why do we believe spiritual people are unflappable? Why do we think spiritual people spend their days in peaceful bliss, meditating, doing yoga, and feeling compassion for all beings 24/7?

This kind of spirituality is sold in magazines, through gurus, and at retreats with promises of everlasting forgiveness, personal transformation, and transcendence in a gourd of ayahuasca. But I'm not buying it. Spirituality is tough. It's dirty, and it's struggle. If not for that, we would be content to sit on our asses all day, drinking kombucha and chanting in enlightened voices.

In Ecuador, something breaks open. It unleashes the swear words and my passion for living life fully—with a touch of recklessness that had never been there before. I no longer care about being liked. I speak forcefully when required. The "nice girl" begins to disappear. The sun rises each morning, its rays coming through the window and slapping me awake, daring me to engage another day full-out by receiving everything it offers, whether it's the workers showing up drunk or my neighbor gifting us a juicy papaya.

I learn to be fluid with everything. Impermanence becomes a way of life, not simply a concept. Non-attachment is a survival mechanism, not a Buddhist philosophy.

I also interact with my environment differently than I have in the past, and I pay more attention. I am acutely aware of life's tiniest details. I walk the property noticing that buds have turned into small limes, and what I thought was a few twigs has become home to local finches. From our hill, I watch the ocean tides, waves smashing against rocks, and local fishing boats coming in and going out. Everything has its natural rhythm, unencumbered by alarm clocks, agendas, and meetings. I now feel when I am hungry, sleepy, or need to move my body. I discover that I, too, have a rhythm. It feels so good allowing it to dictate my time and how I use my energy.

As I gain strength in the external world, I defer to Napo for approval of my spiritual journey. I still believe he is the one who will show me the way through a maze of shamanism to recover the soul that I lost at birth, the one seeking unity and communion with the divine.

As the seasons pass, I surrender my power to him. He becomes a taskmaster even as he deals with his own demons. Daily, he takes out his frustration on me. We have each other as mirrors; the other reflects what we don't want to see in ourselves.

In Napo, I see a distortion of the masculine as his machismo culture surfaces in our daily lives. In me, he sees his repressed feminine aspect being whipped into submission. We dance a terrible dance together when before we had danced in harmony, sharing our energy instead of fighting.

Gradually, I lose myself in his world. There are days when I simply cry myself to sleep, afraid that I have made the biggest mistake of my life. Yet there are other moments when the simple act of harvesting the fruit from our land opens me to a deep connection to all of life that I can only define as transcendent. I am caught in two worlds, never knowing which one will appear. I continue dancing between light and shadow, the physical and metaphysical worlds, and my inner and outer experiences.

In the morning, the birds wake me with their joyous songs, their tweets vibrating the energy of a new possibility. As much as I revel in these morning hours, I love the quiet just before night arrives even more. The birds sing a different melodious tune, as if they are attuned to the inevitable darkness. The light shines unobtrusively at twilight, complementing their lullabies. I love the glow that portends the dark blanket holding the stars as they twinkle reverently in the universe.

I often wake up in the middle of the night and walk outside to allow the full moon or the glow of constellations to illuminate my soul. I feel safe in this twilight, surrounded by a cosmic energy that seems like home. The night becomes my refuge during the intense years after I settle in Ecuador. At first, everything begins to change. Then, as if an earthquake were shaking the ground, I feel the tremors of my life collapsing into itself.

Napo and I argue more and more. With each argument, he gets more aggressive and hurtful. He claims he does it to disturb my ego and couches the discussion as part of my apprenticeship. I rebel against his perception, calling out the machismo aspect of trying to control me.

After one especially heated argument, I leave the property and walk twenty minutes to the ocean. I feel an irresistible pull toward the water as I approach the beach. I intuitively know that my healing is in the sea. Leaving my towel and clothes on the beach, I run into the waves and allow them to embrace me as I dive down. Wave after wave, I go deeper, until my feet barely touch the bottom. One more dive, and I stay under the water. I crouch down, holding on to the sand and listening to the sound of a muffled roar overhead. I don't want to surface. I feel safe here, calm and loved.

I have the sensation of disintegrating and feel myself breaking apart in these waters. Years before, I had felt the same pull toward the ocean, a compelling invitation to silence and peace when I thought I had lost everything I loved.

Although death did not win that night in Maine, in 2009, I was branded with a memory of the seduction, which rises in the night's silence, calling to me in the most challenging times. In these moments, I feel the breakdown is upon me; I want to flee and throw myself into the ocean, engulfed by waves that will bring the promise of peace and silence to fruition. But I choose life over and over again.

As I crouch under the ocean waves on a shore far from Maine, I wonder if some part of me has taken that final step into the dark waters. I wonder whether time and space are playing a trick on me. Perhaps I feel the relief and calm I sought years ago.

My lungs plead for air. Seizing the tranquility the ocean has gifted me, I rise above the waves and swim for shore, fully choosing to continue the path placed before me.

I wonder about the difference between breaking down and breaking open. There is a kind of dying that is not physical but is real nevertheless. Does death follow us from the day we are born, nudging us to fulfill our life's potential, daring us to be more as the sand in our hourglass slowly runs out? Can an intimacy with death make him an ally instead of a specter, galvanizing the human fear of the unknown? Should we look over our shoulders as we walk hand in hand with life, afraid that this shadowy figure might reach us before we feel complete and whole?

I don't know the answers to these questions, but I have learned that there is a price to pay for choosing life. By the time death arrives to collect his due, I'll be ready, knowing that I resolved to face life with open arms, received what came toward me, and used it to be the creative force in my life.

— 21 —
THE DAY THE DREAM DIES

December is supposed to be a month of joy, singing, and family. Long dinners with traditional foods—empanadas, croquetas, and wine. The anticipation of presents being torn open under a Douglas fir that smells of the forest, decorated with blinking, colored lights and tinsel that reflects their hues.

It is supposed to be a warm house filled with the scent of apple pie, pine, and brewing coffee. Voices shouting, laughing, and teasing as we tell stories to playfully embarrass one another and reminisce about past times.

It isn't supposed to be a time of loss, pain, and distance. It isn't supposed to be a story of breaking down and breaking open. It isn't supposed to hurt.

December 8, 2017, is a night I will never forget.

It started when Napo missed his late-November flight to the United States because he didn't have the original version of an immigration document. He had taken a duplicate to the airport because he didn't want to lose it. I had read online that a photocopy was acceptable. It wasn't.

He called me from Quito when he couldn't board. It was midnight. I spoke to the agent but could not convince her to allow him onto the plane. He was furious.

He returned to the Oasis a few days later, livid and on a tear. He wouldn't look at me for days, and we only spoke when we had to.

On the evening of December 8, 2017, I clean the kitchen after dinner and Napo begins drinking *puntas*, a grain alcohol that Americans call moonshine. With each glass, he becomes more drunk and aggressive. This isn't the first time. He has begun drinking excessively over the past few months. He can't hold his liquor, and *puntas* is as raw as alcohol gets before you use it as lighter fluid.

I am closing my laptop when he slams his fist on the desk. "You purposely fucked up my flights. What's wrong with you, stupid woman? Can't you do anything right? You are a cunt, a useless being."

I brace myself. I start to get up from the chair, but he pushes me down.

"Get on that stupid machine and book me a flight now. I want to get out of here."

I say nothing and check Delta flights. They cost thousands of dollars and have limited availability until January.

"There's nothing available now for less than two thousand dollars. The first flights where you could use the ticket voucher are in January," I report. "I can book those tomorrow." I start getting up from my chair, trying to get to the bedroom door before he reaches me.

He flies at me and pushes me hard. I feel a sudden uncontrollable surge of rage, not anger but sheer red-like-fire rage. That push stands in for every push I have ever experienced in my life. Every person who has tried to control, diminish, hurt, or lord over me is behind that push. Rage surges like a fierce dragon coming out from its lair, now awakened after a long sleep, enraged that someone has dared to open the door. I strike him to push him away so I can run. He falls back, surprised that I have defended myself. His face is crimson, and drool drips from his mouth. He morphs into a monster set to destroy me.

I am cornered between the desk and the wall. When Napo's fist hits me, I barely have enough time to block it from reaching my face.

The impact lands near my ear. He then grabs my hair, shakes my head violently, makes me lose my balance, and crashes my skull against the wall. I fall into the chair, vaguely hearing his curses and feeling his slaps. I am dizzy and the room looks fuzzy. With another slap, I surface from my semi-conscious state.

"You will do what I say! You will obey me! You will book that flight now, not tomorrow!"

"You need to call your brother to calm down," I say, my mind kicking into gear to deflect his attention. "Call Carlos." His brother is my only hope for stopping this rampage.

Incredibly, Napo does what I say. He has the phone on speaker. Carlos answers, concerned. "What happened, brother?" he says, alarmed by Napo's slurring voice.

"Alicia is a bitch; she is stupid. She needs to be dominated to obey. She can't even book my flights after she screwed them up. She is a psychopath. All messed up, deranged!" He wobbles on his feet, yelling into the phone like it's a megaphone.

"Calm down, brother. Of course she is deranged. We knew that. Did you hurt her? Don't hurt her, or she will make trouble for you and the family."

At that moment, I know where I stand. And it's on shaky ground. All the past arguments, insults, and threats become an avalanche coming straight for me. I have nowhere to run. The only thing that saves me is my anger channeling into my mind, sorting the chaos, managing my fear, and moving my fragmented thoughts into a cohesive plan to survive that night.

Carlos makes Napo promise not to hurt me, but the damage has been done. Napo pushes me onto the chair. "Now! Book the flights, now," he demands. I book the flights as he keeps drinking and raging. I close the laptop, grab my phone, and take them with me when I escape to the bedroom and lock the door.

I sit on the bed and cry. I have become a victim. For years, I had worked with domestic violence victims but could never have predicted that I would be here, locked in my room, with a madman outside the door threatening to kill me.

With every breath, I open my chest to inhale and exhale deeply, calming my nervous system. Then I go to work. "You've got this," I say between sobs, as if I am talking to a client. "You've got this. You know what to do. Get a grip."

I take photographs of the bruises on my face, arms, and chest. I have always bruised easily, so the purple-and-blue bruises pop onto the canvas of my skin as if a painter has spattered his pigments, defacing his work of art. I shove the painful emotions down deep so they won't interfere with what I know I have to do.

I upload my photos to the cloud as Napo begins banging on the door in addition to threatening and insulting me. The bedroom has two exits—the door to the kitchen and the window. I don't have the strength to climb out the window.

Through the door, his anger rages. Insults, threats, and promises to destroy me echo off the wood panels. We have three couples living on the property, Workaway volunteers from Poland, France, and England who work half days in exchange for lodging. They stay in the house next door. If they can hear him, they don't come to investigate.

I turn on my iPhone's recording app and capture Napo's angry threats until his phone rings. It's Carlos calling to make sure Napo has calmed down. I can hear them talking through the door but can't distinguish what they say. I shut off the recording and lie back on the bed. Sleep couldn't be more welcome. Lying under the mosquito net, I hear the soft buzzing of an errant mosquito and think, *I wonder how he got in here.* Then the veil of darkness overtakes me.

The following day, I clean myself up, use makeup to cover the bruises on my face, take a deep breath, and unlock the bedroom door. I have no idea what I will find.

Napo sits at the kitchen table, having his tea and a boiled egg. He has already been outside getting the workers settled into the day's chores. At first, he doesn't look up.

The kitchen is a mess. Dirty plates and broken glass lie in the sink. Napo also looks like hell, his long hair disheveled and knotted. He wears gym workout pants, a matching jacket, and an old T-shirt. He hasn't changed his daily workout clothes in several days. He smells of sweat, dirt, and bitterness.

I put the kettle on to make my coffee. One of the Workaway volunteers knocks on the open door. Leaning in, he says, "We're going to Puerto Lopez to the market this morning so we don't miss the fresh produce. We'll finish our work in the afternoon if that's okay."

I need to get away from Napo for the day and see my opportunity. A large bump developed overnight, replacing my normal bicep muscle with a swollen lump. I also woke up dizzy and know I have a concussion. I need to see a doctor.

Before Napo can answer, I say, "Sure. That's fine. I'll go with you. I also have to go into town."

"Great. Let's leave in thirty minutes," the volunteer suggests.

"I'll be ready," I answer. "I'll come over to your house."

I drink my coffee and eat a stale bread roll to get something into my stomach. I pick up my backpack and get ready to leave the house, but Napo blocks the exit. I am stuck between the living room couch and the door.

"It's not over, Alicia. You will listen to what I tell you. If you think you can control me, you are wrong. I will do what I want. This is Ecuador. You don't know what it can be like. No one will believe you." He pushes me onto the couch and raises his hand to hit me.

For a brief moment, time stands still. I am surprisingly relaxed, perhaps resigned. Everything happens in slow motion. Before his hand makes its descent, I hear a voice in my ear, loud and forceful, that shakes me out of my stupor.

"*Grite, hija, grite!*" Scream, daughter, scream!

It's my mother's voice, as insistent and loud as if she were standing next to me.

In that split second, I realize she is giving me a weapon—my voice, a weapon many women don't use. Our silence is a deal we make with our abusers. We always get the short end of that deal. Our power lies in making noise. My mother knew this.

So I scream as loud as I can. "Help me! He's hitting me! Help me!"

Napo is so startled that his arm stops midair, allowing me to jump off the couch and run out the door with my backpack. I'm still screaming. "Help me!"

The volunteers run out of the building next door. I am crying. One of the women grabs me, embraces me, and helps me up the stairs into their house. Napo comes outside, shaking his head, looking down, and muttering, "It's not like that. It's not like that at all." He keeps walking and goes up to the terrace to meet one of the workers. He undoubtedly heard me scream too.

Marline, the French girl, sits on the couch with me as I cry and shake. Monica, the Polish woman, older than the others, gets me a glass of water and sits before me.

"What happened, Alicia?" Monica asks with concern in her voice as she holds my trembling hand.

I tell them what happened last night and this morning. The men stay away, sensing this conversation is something only women can engage in. One of them stands at the door looking out.

"My father used to hit my mother," confesses Marline. "I watched it happen, which I think is why I'm the way I am. I'm independent and will not let anyone tell me what to do. I think that keeps me away from having good relationships, unfortunately. It is something I have to work on every day."

"This doesn't happen to me, not me," I tearfully plead. "I'm the one who's supposed to be strong, the one who defends others. I'm the one who helps others save themselves. This doesn't happen to me!" I cry, rejecting the victimhood that threatens to seep into my being.

Monica adds, "There is no reason for a man to hit a woman. This is unacceptable. Every couple has problems, but this is not how to solve them. What can we do to help?"

"I need to go to Puerto Lopez to the clinic to see a doctor," I say, showing them my bruised arm. "From there, I don't know what I'll do."

We leave the property. I know my brain is scrambled when I pay the driver five dollars for a three-dollar fare and walk away without the change. I don't remember giving him the money until the taxi leaves and a volunteer asks why I didn't take the change.

At the clinic, I say I fell while hiking. The nurse and doctor exchange knowing glances. I feel embarrassed and exposed. I never would have imagined myself excusing physical violence with a lie. How many women have done this? So many. Now I am one of them.

I can't reconcile the strong, confident Alicia whose life's work is supporting others in their fight for authenticity and agency with the Alicia whose body is painted in tattoo-like bruises and who lies on the cot getting an antibiotic shot in the ass.

This will not be the last time Napo is violent or abusive. Even so, I stay with him and become better at protecting myself. The moment he raised his hand to me, he destroyed everything. At that moment, I began to leave emotionally, mentally, and physically. And finally, spiritually. But it will take another year to find enough courage, resilience, and faith in myself to leave him once and for all.

There is a certain kind of loneliness that crosses the line into desperation. It is a loneliness born of becoming invisible. You don't belong where you thought you belonged, and you believe you cannot escape or find your place of belonging.

It's a kind of loneliness where you feel threatened by the world surrounding you. You're constantly vigilant for any sign that you are in danger. If you must interact with people, you wear the secret mask that you keep in the nightstand, the one with the pasted-on smile and dull, lifeless eyes.

This loneliness is born in betrayal. The dream you thought would save you vanishes like the footprints you leave on the beach. The tide of time washes away any trace of your existence. The one you love becomes your crucible. The tender, wise, loving man becomes a dark and enraged monster. You don't recognize yourself as your hair begins to fall out, your muscles weaken from lack of food, and your mind can't focus because you no longer serve any purpose.

You're told repeatedly that you don't matter. You're told that you're stupid, that your decisions are wrong, and that your reality is a fable. Every failure is your fault. If he hits you, it's because you made him. He was defending himself against a psychopath. You're told that no one is coming to help.

He monitors your phone calls, except when you escape to a small, damp alcove that he doesn't know about. It's in an unfinished cement building. In the dead of night, you sneak out of the house with your aguardiente, relief in a glass, to commune with the moon, stars, and night animals, simply to remember that you're alive and must save your sanity.

But there is always the spark, *la lucesita*, that refuses to be extinguished. It no longer burns brightly, but it is constant. The light in your soul reminds you of who you are and tells you that you matter. It is the umbilical cord to the universal movement, the cosmos, and the Creator. It is the divine spark that will one day save your life.

– 22 –
THE SPIRITS ARE ANGRY

We built Quinta Oasis on land with a formidable ancestral history that made it home to spirits and energies. The local people still retain many of the physical characteristics and traditions of the early Manteño civilization. I often wonder if the land called to us, seeking a shamanic steward that would revitalize the earth, which had grown fallow.

Although I was raised to consider apparitions normal, I have never experienced the heightened metaphysical wars that shamans deal with. Unseen, opposing forces inhabit the land at Quinta Oasis, causing accidents and death. Once, when Carlos visits, birds begin dropping from the sky. Napo and Carlos are visibly alarmed. They make me leave the property as they conduct a shamanic clearing. I go into town for the day, but the clearing takes thirty days to complete. What occurs on the thirtieth night confirms how tangible metaphysical forces can be.

Today has been busy. My body is sore from pruning trees, weeding, and carrying wood for the grill in the outdoor kitchen. An evening dip in the pool relaxes me, and soon I am asleep, protected from buzzing insects by the mosquito net over the bed.

After months of sleeping in the other room, Napo has returned to our bed. I relented to his pleas when I noticed he wasn't sleeping well.

Carlos is still staying on the property, and Napo doesn't want him to see that we are no longer together. Tonight, Napo is beside me when a loud boom shakes me awake. He does not stir, and I investigate without waking him.

It's almost as bright as daylight outside. The full moon's soft glow causes the palm trees' shadows to dance in the breeze. Nature's music—trilling insects and singing frogs—fills the empty spaces. Bella and Chief run back and forth in a game of tag as they follow me up to the terrace level. The outdoor kitchen is lit in a greenish hue as the moonlight seeps through the green-tinted plastic roofing. I conduct a short inspection of the property from my perch in the kitchen, but it yields no clues about the booming sound. *Tomorrow, I'll tell Napo about the noise, and maybe we'll discover the source*, I think as I return to the house.

I'm on the brick path outside the house when I turn to look at the moon one last time. "You're so beautiful," I whisper to her, expecting my words of appreciation to journey to the cosmos. Slowly, I turn and take a step forward.

Without warning, an unseen force violently pushes me sideways. Only two meters or so exist between the path and the house's solid brick wall. I fall toward it in slow motion, as if I'm outside my body. I calculate where to step to slow my trajectory. I look at the freshly weeded ground and manage two steps before I hit the wall. The second step reduces my speed enough that I can raise my arms and stretch out my hands to buffer the blow from my body hitting the house. Then there is another push with a force that makes my arms buckle as my head snaps forward and hits the bricks. Everything goes dark.

I wake with dirt in my mouth and blood in my eyes. My dogs stand over me protectively, and Chief snarls at something I can't see. Bella whines and nuzzles me, covering me with her body. I pass out again.

Then someone picks me up from the ground. "Alicia, Alicia, stand up. Don't go to sleep. Stand up!" It's Napo. The barking dogs under the bedroom window have woken him. I struggle to stand. He helps me inside and into the bed with instructions not to fall asleep. He leaves, then returns with a glass of water and places a bag of frozen peas on my head. "What happened?" he asks, concerned.

"I don't know," I mumble. "There was a boom . . ."

The following day, I awaken to voices in the kitchen. Napo and Carlos are eating breakfast and discussing what happened. I stumble out of the bedroom, my hands sliding along the walls to help me maintain my balance. When they see me, they exchange glances that tell me I must look like hell. Napo helps me to the kitchen table and makes me tea.

"I didn't hear anything last night, not even the dogs," says Carlos. "Why were you outside at that hour?" There's a hint of accusation in his voice.

"I heard a loud boom and went outside to investigate. Napo was asleep, and I didn't want to wake him," I say defensively. My head is throbbing. I rub my temples to ease the pain and discover a lump the size of an egg on my forehead.

"You need to ice that today. Your eyes look like a raccoon," says Napo jokingly.

I don't see the humor in it and grunt my displeasure before sipping my tea. "Can you tell me what happened?" My question is directed to both of them.

Carlos begins to explain. "Do you remember thirty days ago when we did a shamanic clearing of the property? Yesterday was the thirtieth day. The boom you heard is the noise spirits make when they leave the plasma, like a sonic boom. But they were angry. They cannot hurt us because we are shamans. But they tried to kill you to punish us before they left." Napo nods in agreement as he breaks open his hard-boiled egg.

"I have told you, Alicia, that your life is intertwined with mine,"

Napo remarks, still eating his breakfast. "And sometimes this can be dangerous. The metaphysical world is real, and good and bad energies will affect us. After today, the property will have good energy. Carlos and I will do one more ceremony today. You must stay indoors until we are done."

I spend the day in bed, alternating the bag of peas with ice on my forehead. My eyes blacken for days, making it appear as if I've been in a fight. I keep my sunglasses on so no one will notice or make up stories about the lump on my forehead and my swollen eyes.

A week later, Napo and I have breakfast on the kitchen terrace. It rained the night before. Although the ground has turned into a muddy mix, the sun is already baking it dry. The scent of ocean salt and bougainvillea blossoms floats in the air. The dogs play near us. One of the workers has already begun to trim the palm trees. "This is what it is like when energy is clean," Napo remarks. "From now on, I'll conduct monthly ceremonies to maintain this positive aspect of our land."

Unfortunately, the following year will bring more struggle. As the property develops, inviting visitors from around the globe, darkness descends and absorbs any light the shaman might bring.

There are months when we are apart. I am required to spend time in Ecuador because of my resident status, and Napo needs to do the same in the United States. We have hired Alejandro and his wife as the property's caretakers to do maintenance and upkeep. Nevertheless, the property requires that one of us always be there.

I don't mind being alone on the property. It is peaceful, and I am busy with the land and odd jobs I want to complete. The larger building is almost finished. On the ground floor, where we plan to have a community room, Napo had an artist create a mural representing *Pachakutic*. In Quechua, an Indigenous language, *Pachakutic* is the word used for a creation myth based on pre-Colombian Andean cultures. It involves the cycles of life and death and changes in the sun and movement of the earth, bringing a new era of consciousness. Napo claims we are already experiencing these shifts, both as individuals and collectively.

Two walls in the community room are blank, and I decide to spend my time painting symbols on them. The first is a colorful, abstract kneeling figure with its hands folded as if in prayer. It might be interpreted as a Buddha or a shaman. The other is the *chakana*, the Andean cross symbolizing the elements and three shamanic levels: the underworld, the earth, and the heavens. I want this room to be a sacred space where guests meditate, practice yoga, and engage in conversations that bring people together. The images I paint contain the intention of healing and evolution.

Each mural takes a week to complete. I light palo santo in the room, take up the brushes and acrylics, and lose myself in creating the paintings. Like writing, art provides moments of immersion into my inner world, bringing me joy and peace.

Unbeknownst to Napo, I host retreats at the property when he is away. These events nourish my spirit and keep me connected to my purpose. I save the money, sensing that I will one day need the funds to support myself.

Occasionally, Workaway volunteers also find a home with me on the property. They are typically young (but not always) and curious. I like having them, not only because we need the labor but also because I enjoy learning about their cultures and dreams. I also enjoy their boundless energy and stories of world travel. They keep me company and preserve my sanity. To this day, I am still in contact with many volunteers who stayed during my time at Quinta Oasis.

If there is one thing I learn from living in Ecuador, it is that life is a series of checks and balances. For every difficult moment, there is a moment of exquisite joy. Brilliant dawns follow dark and moonless nights. A kind word counters any evil intention. And for every death, there is life.

In 2018, Lula has a litter of puppies under our house. We took her in when a neighbor abandoned her. I hear the puppies' cries under the house as they nurse and grow. I feel privileged that Lula allows me under the house with her puppies. I name each one despite knowing that I cannot keep them all: Li'l Dude, Peanut, Bandit, Pebbles, Yogi. I choose one to keep and name her Sophie, a reminder of the goddess Sophia, who I sense in my inner psyche. Sophie is still with me today, a reminder of the inner spirit that continues to guide me.

Yet there are also difficult moments. A bittersweetness descends upon me as I gaze out over the ocean in the evenings, alone in my house with only the dogs as company. I feel lost and afraid of the future. I still don't realize that a woman alone on a property might also be a target. Between the caretaker's family, the dogs, and a revolver in the nightstand, I naively perceive that I am safe. Yet the unexpected often intrudes into my peaceful moments.

Today I begin my day, as always, with a cup of strong coffee. I awaken later than usual. The heat is already rising. I wrap my silk robe around me instead of the terry cloth one that keeps me warm. As my second cup brews, I am drawn to the balcony, intending to sit outside with my coffee.

I unlatch the door and jiggle it to slide it open. Suddenly, I feel a slap on my right shoulder. I turn to look directly at a giant tarantula, larger than my hand, that has landed just below my shoulder joint. Its body is a deep purple, and it is covered in tiny barbed hairs that it will launch when threatened—I know this from experience. Its dark brown legs extend over my shoulder blade, its little feet penetrating my silk robe to my skin. An inaudible scream catches in my throat and gags me. "Stay calm. Stay calm," I whisper as I furiously attempt to untie the robe. I walk the room in circles with the spider's weight on my shoulder as it clings tighter. My trembling fingers catch in the silk ribbon, and instead of loosening it, I make it tighter. Finally, the ribbon around my waist slackens. I pull the robe off my back, step out of it, and cover the creature so it doesn't escape. I run out of the house screaming, "*Alejandro, Alejandro, Dios mío!*"

The caretaker must think I am crazy when I arrive at his door and babble. I drag him by the arm to the house and point to the robe that lies in a pile on the floor. "It's there, under the robe. Please get it out of here!" Alejandro gingerly picks it up and finds the tarantula still clinging to the silk. He forms a pouch with the robe and takes it far into the garden, where he kills it. When he returns the robe, it is marked with a blue liquid. I'd like to think the tarantula was equally afraid and peed itself. I tell Alejandro to throw the robe in the garbage.

Do we ever understand how resilient we are? Perhaps we underestimate our capacity to adapt when we are comfortably ensconced in a culture that dictates how we spend our hours, our days, and, eventually, our lives. Is courage something that arises when events demand something more from us than we ever thought possible? It lies latent, a warrior who has spent days readying herself for the extraordinary moment that calls her forth to save those she loves, to save herself.

I am reminded of a quote attributed to Chögyam Trungpa: "To be a spiritual warrior, one must have a broken heart; without a broken heart and the sense of tenderness and vulnerability, your warriorship is untrustworthy."

Ecuador has awoken the spiritual warrior in me by breaking my heart open. From shamanic warfare to an enlightened approach to love, my years with Napo have taught me that I am much more than I ever believed. Now, I see *la lucesita*, the divine spark, in myself and others. Still, I remain ever vigilant of my desire to close my heart when I'm afraid.

The path of the spiritual warrior is a path of surrender, not struggle against. It's a path of acceptance, not will. It's a path of love, not war. Because the goal of the spiritual warrior is unity with peace and the divine, the only road to peace is through spirituality. When the warrior in me surrenders to the fact that anything I fight is a projection, I discover peace comes from a feeling of love, compassion, tenderness, and unity. This is the true path of the spiritual warrior, and I can forge the path anew.

There is no slaying of dragons and no heroic episode; I must only recognize that if there is a dragon, I am the dragon, and the story is an illusion I created. It has taken time for me to realize my spiritual path is based on surrendering to what is genuine and present right now, in the face of all the stories I have crafted and those others have created for me and which I have embraced. The only way to grow spiritually is to give myself over to something greater than myself that cannot be defined.

Still, despite my illusions, something deeper remains consistent and persistent. My consciousness continues to expand with the events of my life, the successes and the failures, the joys and the sorrows. My consciousness integrates the lessons I learn and, no matter what, constantly renews itself—because *that* consciousness exists beyond me, and always has, and always will.

– 23 –
HOLDING HANDS WITH THE DEVIL

When I was a little girl in Catholic school, the nuns taught us to say the rosary. Every morning, we would begin our day with a prayer. If we were disobedient, it was common for the nuns to send us into a little corner equipped with a small kneeler to say the rosary as penance. I used to think they used the rosary to wipe away any original sin we'd carried into this life from birth. I must have left that school sparkling clean.

It wasn't long before saying the rosary took on another meaning for me. Perhaps it was my way of coping during the many times I was shoved into the corner because they mistook my misunderstanding of the language and cultural rules for disobedience. I took solace in prayer. The repetition was soothing, like a mantra or a song. Time would stand still as I lifted my gaze to the heavens, tiny beads held gently between my fingers with the length of the pearl rosary running down my jumper, marking the passage of minutes I could not remember.

In Ecuador, the days are my rosary. I begin every day by offering a silent prayer to the Creator. It keeps me grounded in my struggle to regain authorship of my life as we build the brick and stone that becomes Quinta Oasis, which I now view as Napo's temple. There are a few good days when we converse and laugh like before. Mostly, there are days when his moods hover over me like a dark and ominous cloud, an unspoken threat.

With each prayer, I imagine myself closer to freedom, even though I don't know what that looks like. I won't realize until much later that I began my relationship with Napo not as a partner, as I had imagined, but more as an acolyte that he wanted to form in his image. It was like fitting a square peg in a round hole.

He continues to have angry fits and deliver hours-long litanies of my failures. I tune him out. When he becomes threatening, I secretly turn on my phone's recording function, anticipating that I might need proof one day. Because, as he says, we are in Ecuador, and who would believe me?

I call him a monster on the day he strikes me. He hates that word. He blames me for his violence, claiming he hits me to defend himself against my psychopathy (his word). My daily prayer keeps me alive. It protects my delicate soul, which seeks healing and love but has wandered into the path of a shaman. What have I learned?

You have to meet the Devil to know that God is within you.

As my outer world crumbles, my inner world strengthens. With the help of a few good friends, to whom I confess my predicament and who safeguard the file with the evidence of his violence, I recover my courage and confidence. He does his best to keep me from reaching out, but I still secretly call my friends from the alcove in the unfinished building to report that I am alive and determined. But I haven't figured out how to leave.

My dream of a life in Ecuador, working side by side with a wisdom keeper, creating a refuge where others come to heal their souls, dies a little bit each day. But I'm not ready to give up yet.

The dirt is still damp. Last night's rain soaked the land before the morning sunshine began baking the earth, slowly drying what had been covered with moisture. I'm still in my pajamas as I walk down my home's concrete stairs to meet my four dogs, Chief, Bella, Lula, and now Sophie, Lula and Chief's pup. These animals now call my home their home too.

The nearby keyhole garden, with its circular brick wall, beckons to me. Bella runs over to sniff around the base. It appears we had visitors last night. Her nose catches a whiff of the scent left behind by a nocturnal creature that helped itself to the carrots that had begun emerging from the rich soil.

My fingers impose themselves on the roots below to see if any carrots escaped the little creature's greedy escapade. A few earthworms come to the surface, as if complaining about my intrusion.

The basil begins to flower as the plants threaten to take over most of the circular garden. It's time to pinch the blossoms so the earth's energy flows to the fragrant leaves that will eventually flavor my dishes. I work carefully around the plants, squeezing fervently so they don't go to seed.

The basil leaves' oily sweetness coats my fingers, which I bring close to my face. Dirt seems to be forever stuck between the soft pads of my fingers and the cracked nails, now ragged and short from digging in the soil. "It looks like a dirt tattoo instead of the French manicures I'm used to," I comment aloud, as if I'm having a conversation with someone.

The soil has become part of my being, as have other natural elements. I depend on the rains to quench the thirst of the fruit trees that now produce sweet oranges, tart lemons, bright red cherries, and giant bunches of bananas. The coconut palms are heavy with hairy orbs filled with sweet milk and delicious white meat. Everywhere there are the smells and sounds of life bursting from above and below. I pause and relish this moment, close my eyes, and allow the gentle breeze and the morning sunshine to wash over me, warming my body and nourishing my soul.

I remember feeling this way when I was a little girl helping my father in the yard or my mother in the garden. But as years passed, other things became more important—school, work, and career. I lost touch with that joyful sensation of being outdoors. Only for a few moments, watching a sunset or paddling on the Chesapeake Bay, would I reconnect to that sensation of peace, only to again be absorbed into my busy daily life.

Ecuador has rekindled my desire for a deeper connection to the land and the ocean. There is an ache inside me that is only relieved when I walk barefoot on the dirt or swim in the sea. I find a tranquil respite by diving below the water's surface and listening to the thunder of waves above while I am enveloped in nature's amniotic fluid. It's a reminder that every moment, like every wave, comes and goes, never to return in precisely the same way. The ocean gives me hope that I will navigate rough waters until I rest in a serene harbor, safe from the storms that threaten to drown me.

– 24 –
ESCAPE

It has been four years since I first started traveling to Ecuador to be with Napo. My moods swing from joy and peace to struggle and fear. I came to build a dream, a retreat center, with a man who had unexpectedly entered my life. He is a sixth-generation shaman whom I met through a friend. I fell hard for his message of redemption and communion with the sacred, promising to reconcile my spiritual quest, which began at birth. He was supposed to be my protector, navigator, teacher, and partner. But in Ecuador, he changed from the man I loved to a monster I must now survive. On a whim, I made a decision that changed the course of my life. Now I know that I chose a dangerous path without understanding the consequences.

I return to the United States for Christmas in 2018. I spend part of the week with family and friends in Boston and the rest of the time in Annapolis with my son and his father. Through the eyes of those who love me, I begin to reconnect with the person I used to be. That trip gives me the strength and confidence to leave Napo and save my life.

I celebrate my birthday with friends and family in Boston. It's as if the past is a high-speed train that meets the station in the present moment. We gather at a local restaurant, each person at the table representing a slice of my story. My sister and brother are there—I'm seeing them for the first time in two years. They hold a different story about who I am than my friends do. Karen and her husband Jim join us. I worked for Karen at the beginning of my meeting planning career. We saw each other through work challenges, career milestones, births, divorces, and deaths. Gerry S., my best friend from college, also arrives to celebrate with me. I nicknamed him the Marlboro Man when we were freshmen because of his tall build and good looks. He was my lifeline when my father died. Our stories are intertwined from our college years until the present, although now at a distance.

Gradually, as the evening progresses, I begin to remember the person I had been. Reminiscing about past times floods my mind with memories and sensations that initially feel like they belong to someone else. The evening is bittersweet as I compare the identity I've forged in Ecuador with the woman who achieved anything she put her mind to.

I go on to spend Christmas in Annapolis with my son and his father. Sitting under the twinkling lights of the Christmas tree, drinking spiked eggnog, and laughing at bad jokes and tales of our youth is the best gift I could receive. Being close to my son again breaks my heart open with the depth of love I feel for him. I simply want to hold him as if I will never let go.

In the stillness of Christmas night, I light a fire while the others sleep. Warmed by the flames—and whiskey—I listen to my heart. I feel the time is approaching when I can be courageous and confident enough to find safety within myself and leave Napo. I can no longer bear the arguments, the physical threats, and the gaslighting that keep me a prisoner on my land. I dread what could happen if I stay. I know I am disappearing like a tiny spark the breeze intends to extinguish. The person I had been is determined to keep that spark burning.

It is New Year's Eve 2018, entering 2019. An airline pilot and his two children are staying at the property. He invites Napo and me to the terrace for a drink to celebrate the New Year. I leave after two drinks, but Napo stays with him until almost midnight. When he returns to the house, he is utterly inebriated and paranoid, claiming I had been flirting with the pilot.

"What are you saying?" I try to reason with him. "I left after two drinks, and you are the one who stayed."

"I saw how he looked at you, and you responded! I can't trust you," he yells, his face flushed with anger. Across the room, he holds a drink in his hand, unsteady on his feet.

I quickly lock myself in the bedroom, anticipating his violence. As he bangs on the door, cursing and threatening me, I methodically pack a small bag with clothes and put my laptop and chargers into a backpack. I call his brother, telling him to call Napo and calm him down.

"You two have to figure out your relationship," Carlos responds, annoyed at my call. "I cannot be your marriage counselor!"

With astounding clarity, I reply, "You are absolutely right, Carlos. And I promise you, tomorrow, I will resolve this. But now, please call Napo and calm him down. He is drunk, angry, and violent." At that moment, I know I must leave the next day, even if it means abandoning everything I have worked for.

Napo's phone rings and I hear him talking to Carlos, slurring his words but listening to his brother's advice. The banging on the door ceases. After some shuffling sounds, the house becomes silent. I lie in bed staring at the ceiling fan, counting the *click, click* sounds of the fan's hanging chains hitting each other until I fall asleep.

In the morning, sunshine pours through the shutters, waking me slowly. As if following a script I don't question, I shower and dress in a T-shirt, shorts, and sneakers. It's a hot day, and I will be traveling.

I open the shutters and window and drop my backpack and bag onto the ground below. They make a muffled *thump* as they hit the dirt. Closing the window, I pray Napo stays inside. I hear him in the kitchen and prepare to meet him, not knowing what I will find.

When I enter the main room, he is sitting at the table drinking tea and eating a hard-boiled egg and toast, his usual breakfast. He doesn't look up, and I don't say anything. Standing at the counter, I make my coffee and butter a piece of bread.

His curly hair hangs out from under his sweat-stained cap. It's the first time I notice streaks of gray. He wears the same clothes he wore last night. An empty bottle of *puntas* sits on the living room table next to an ashtray and cigarette butt. I suspected he'd started smoking, but this is the first time I find evidence.

"Why don't you sit down? Sit down and eat," he says with a voice as cold as stone. I slowly slide the chair out to sit on the opposite side of the table. "You need to check on our guest today," he says. "I don't want to see him." He still hasn't looked at me.

"I'll do that once I finish my coffee." Ten minutes later, I put the dishes in the sink. "I'm going for a walk around the property, and I'll check in with him." I remain calm, speaking slowly despite the thumping in my chest. I know that as soon as I leave, he will stand at the bedroom door and watch me through the open bedroom window to see where I go.

The dogs are on the porch, and I feel a stab of guilt knowing I am leaving them. "I'll get you later," I promise. I intentionally pause in front of the bedroom window to play with the dogs, and as I anticipated, I see him watching me from the corner of my eye. After a minute, I continue on the path and stop once I'm out of his sight. "One, two, three, four." I finish counting to ten. Then, crouching down, I retrace my steps until I reach the bags below the bedroom window. I carefully stand and peer over the sill, looking through the bedroom to the kitchen. Napo is no longer watching as I sling them over my shoulder.

"Please, God," I plead. "Please don't let him see me walking out and down the hill. Please, God. Please, God," I mutter. I unlock the gate, and as I hug my dogs, I can't hold back the tears. "I'll be back for you, I promise."

I walk down the hill as quickly as I can, occasionally looking back toward the balcony of our house, praying Napo won't go onto it and see me escaping. At the bottom of the hill, I catch a taxi into Puerto Lopez, ten minutes away, and have the driver drop me at the bus station.

Once I have my ticket, I call Anna, the only person in Ecuador I consider a friend. Ever since we met when Napo and I were searching for property, she has been a confidante and her house has been a place where I can relax. When I visited the United States for Christmas, I left a suitcase at her house. "Anna," I said. "I think I'll need to run at some point, and I'll need some clothes. Would you keep the suitcase here?"

"Yes, don't worry," she said. "And if you need a place to stay, I have a guesthouse. You're welcome to stay here if you ever need to." It's time to accept her offer.

When I tell her I'm leaving Napo, she says, "I'll pick you up at the gas station in Puerto Cayo. You can stay in the guesthouse."

I've taken this bus route so many times before. But this time is different. There is no return ticket. Looking out the window as I pass the sea on my left and rickety houses on the right, I vacillate between two competing sensations. The first is fear. What will become of me? I left everything behind, and now what? I have no money, and no one is coming to save me. I'm traveling to an uncertain future, dragging the weight of a man I loved but who could not love me back, a shaman whose power trapped me.

Gradually, the second sensation arises. Freedom. The bus window is open, and the wind blows on my face. Normally, I would close the window. Today, I open it wider, closing my eyes to feel the unlimited possibilities that lie before me. I have no idea where this road leads, but I know there is no returning.

About halfway to Puerto Cayo, my phone begins to vibrate and buzz. I know it's Napo even before I reach for it. When I don't answer, he sends a text: *Where are you? What are you doing?*

I text back, *I'm done. I won't be coming back. Don't try to find me. Don't look for me.* What follows is a cascade of texts, rants, and threats. I imagine his fury at losing control of me. That I would dare leave is unimaginable. He was sure investing in the property and isolating me from friends would keep me "obedient," the word he used when I challenged him.

From January until late February, he sends me threatening emails. I never reply to his calls, texts, or emails. But I do save them as proof should I need to justify why I left. It isn't until early March, when he is calm enough to reason, that I begin communicating with him. When we speak, he is pragmatic. "We have to decide how to manage the Quinta. I don't want to lose the property. We can talk about this."

I must return to take my things and my animals from the property. I enlist Anna's help and her truck, and the same from a man she and I both know to help with the transport. I don't want to go alone.

When we arrive, Napo is waiting with Alejandro, the caretaker. I had kept most of my belongings from the United States in about a dozen shipping boxes, unable to use them on the property. Alejandro helps load the trucks. I remove my art from all the houses and pack my clothes and the other things I need. We fill both trucks.

When it comes time to take the animals, Napo tells me he needs Bella, Chief, and Lula to stay as guard dogs. He allows me to take Sophie and Awki, my cat, the two youngest animals. I'm grateful to Anna for allowing me to bring them.

When I was in my late twenties, I needed to decide where to live and what career to pursue. Once again, a dream provided the answers my mind could not grasp. In the dream, I stood on a cliff with the wind blowing. It had a *Wuthering Heights* feel. I looked into a void, a canyon filled with shadows. Suddenly, a booming voice came across the canyon: "Jump empty-handed into the void. Trust in the universe."

I yelled into the void, "Easy for you to say! You don't have to pay rent!"

That did not deter the voice, which repeated, "Jump empty-handed into the void. Trust in the universe."

I closed my eyes, spread my arms, and jumped into the open space. I didn't fall. My arms became wings, I morphed into an eagle, and the canyon lit up. I was soaring, joyfully free, riding the thermal currents until I awakened, both exhilarated and certain of my next decision.

I have that same feeling once I move into Anna's guesthouse.

Joining Napo in Ecuador was a radical leap, and so is leaving him and everything I have. The universe shows me I've made the right decision. Within three months of leaving Napo and Quinta Oasis, I reignite my business and close more contracts than I have in the previous three years combined. I have grown new wings.

– 25 –
WHAT DOESN'T KILL YOU

Sunset is a paradox. When I watch a sunset, I'm not only holding an ending but also acknowledging a new beginning. This is the continuation of life. A cycle of endings and beginnings, births and deaths, letting go of what no longer serves and moving toward something new. It is the very definition of what the shamans call the universal movement.

Ecuador is a way station on my soul's journey. I once thought it would be my new home, but just as night gives way to day, home is no longer an unmovable place but what we call *caminata*, a trek or long journey with many stops along the way. There is no final destination. Each stop teaches us what we need to know at that moment so we can continue forward. I now believe there is no home to return to, only the home I carry within me on the journey.

I wish the tears would come, the cleansing holy water that brings healing. But they refuse to flow. I'm left with the walls of my heart intact, a dam holding back the inevitable flood begging to be released. My attention to the everyday activities of life keeps me moving forward, pretending I'm okay. Behind the facade, I'm afraid the dam may spring a leak. I fear I might feel the loss, the sadness, the emptiness inside. I long for release, yet it frightens me that I may never resurface from this deep well of grief.

Sadness seeps into the crevices unbidden. The silence becomes my ally. The stars in the heavens call me back. My anger melts as I remember what it feels like to be held, seen, and loved. I am left with my silent prayer, unheeded, waiting for another day, another moment, for the healing to return.

In Puerto Cayo, I begin working again, recovering my income gradually but steadily as the energy in my heart and body heals. I am changed. I am wiser and more compassionate. I am stronger. Clients come to Ecuador to work with me. Through my recovery, I understand my actual work in the world. I reflect on the shamanic teachings Napo shared with me and find peace in my interpretation of these wisdom traditions.

For the next two years, I live in a guesthouse on my friend Anna's property in Puerto Cayo, about forty minutes from Quinta Oasis. I'm forced to interact with Napo to maintain the property. We decide that I will manage the technology and market the property for guest rentals. He will live on the property, assist guests, and maintain it with an on-site worker. Our conversations are never easy. I realize that I suffer from PTSD when every phone call makes my body shake. After I speak with or see him, it takes several days for me to recover from anxiety and panic attacks. Eventually, I maintain minimal contact and stop sending the money he demands.

In September 2019, my fortress comes crashing down. I visit Napo on the property, as I have done several times in the past to discuss maintenance and rentals. Today he is sitting in the outdoor kitchen when I arrive. I am greeted by the dogs, who always enjoy seeing me. I notice they are thin and again feel a stab of guilt and worry, but I must let it pass.

"*Hola*," he says.

"*Hola*," I respond.

His body stiffens, and I intentionally counter, willing my body to relax. We discuss the worker's tasks and Napo's ideas for upkeep. "I'd like to see the second floor of the tall building, Napo. I need photos of it."

"You can't go there. Carlos is staying there and will not allow you to enter." That statement confirms what I have already guessed. I am not the owner and have no rights. I am simply a bank where he goes to withdraw what he needs. I remain silent.

Minutes later, a truck rolls into the property carrying mountains of bricks. "What are all those bricks for?" I ask Napo.

"They are for the bathroom and the rest of the finishes in the penthouse." This is what he calls the second floor of the two-story building.

"I thought we agreed not to finish that floor the traditional way. We agreed to leave it to be finished by a new owner so they could use it as they saw fit."

"I'm finishing it. You are not here. I am. I will do it my way."

"Napo, you've always done it your way. You never listened to me or changed the design based on my requirements. So I shouldn't be surprised that this is another promise you break," I say, anger in my voice.

He ignores my comment and says, "I need two hundred dollars to pay for the bricks."

"Really? Ask Carlos for it since he is enjoying staying there," I angrily reply. I pick up my bag, turn around, and start toward the gate before he can react. I don't look back.

My body is tense during the bus ride back to Puerto Cayo. "How did it go?" Anna asks when I arrive.

"The same as usual. I'm so done."

"You say that, but you keep returning. Why?" Anna never minces words.

"I feel like I've invested so much in that place. Like I have to do something to make sure he doesn't just take it over."

"But Alicia, he has already. You need to let go."

Later that evening, under a full moon, I walk on the beach with a glass of wine. Sophie follows me, both of us dipping our toes in the ocean. I feel something shift in my chest, a kind of unexpected unraveling, like when the noose on a rope comes apart, slowly, then suddenly. My legs become wobbly, and my head feels woozy. I barely make it back to the guesthouse before the grief comes pouring out.

"Oh, my God. This has never been about losing Napo or Quinta Oasis," I cry out loud. "This is about losing a dream, the biggest dream I ever dared to dream. He stole my dream!" I fall to my knees in the kitchen. "He stole my dream!" My body contorts, spilling years of pain onto the floor. I sob for hours, lying on the floor, helpless to stop the emotional tsunami that overwhelms me.

Suddenly, I realize that I have built his dream, not mine. I was deluded into believing the property belonged to both of us. He never considered my ideas or goals and always discounted my hospitality experience and business strategy. Why? Because I was only the bank. The dream I had invested my heart and soul in was a mirage, not an oasis. How could I have been so blind, so naive? I can't bear the shame, the grief, the fear of losing everything, completely disappearing as if I had never existed. Like dominos falling one by one until there is nothing left standing, days pass when I don't see anyone, don't eat, and don't leave the house. I am shattered, broken into tiny pieces, and unable to put myself back together. And that is how I finally begin to heal.

It's taken me years to write this book and find the courage to listen to the voices of my past selves without judgment and regret. At the time, it felt safe to write. Safe behind my computer keys and monitor screen, I could maintain distance and tell the story as if it belonged to someone else. I had no idea what was written in the stars as I waited for my awakening, beyond my resistance and the obvious routines of my human condition.

I stopped writing because the book didn't want to be written, at least not by the person I was becoming. There was more life waiting for me to resolve. My story was, and indeed still is, incomplete.

Years after leaving Napo, I met myself on the other side and have witnessed my growth into the person I am today. Was there struggle? Yes. And I wouldn't change it. Suffering has become a prayer that I offer to the Creator, endowed with a sacredness that transforms pain into compassion and love.

My longing to balance suffering with meaning has grown more pronounced as I age. Through curiosity and with my eyes open, I find transcendental moments amid every experience that poses a duality between light and shadow or ease and difficulty.

There are moments that help us grow beyond our suffering to build an awareness that there is more than what is obvious. These moments teach us that there are no rules to follow except those written within so we can embrace a life of meaning and gratitude generated by the very suffering we so want to avoid.

How curious to discover that the moment I arrived on earth as spirit embodied in a human being, my story began to follow what was written in that unknowable place.

Since birth, I've been seeking God. Not the God of the Bible, the God of the Church, or that white guy with the beard and beatific face that towered over my bed when I was a child dutifully saying my prayers each night.

I'm speaking of the divine energy that is the source of all creation and transcends the material world. The divine consciousness that is always present and that we've lost touch with because of our inability to see with our spiritual eyes what exists beyond empirical knowledge. The energetic source that is immortal and infinite, where death holds no power to destroy, only to transmute. The thing that doesn't die with the people we love because it *is* love, and it is as untouchable as it is sublime. That silent space between the musical notes of the sonata or the quiet moment I've often heard at the ocean when the waves pause momentarily before they storm the beach again. This is the void between the worlds, and this is where consciousness resides. When dancing between the worlds, between the sacred and secular, there is no time or space. They collapse into a singularity, a moment held within the vastness of all experience.

My ever-present longing to merge the sacred with the secular captured me, relentlessly pushing me toward fulfillment and unity between spirit and matter, between human and divine. Through suffering, I learned that enlightenment is not achieved on the mountaintop through chants and a self-imposed exile from the world. The gurus and teachers had misled me. I had abdicated my knowing, a broken vessel leaking my spiritual waters onto barren land.

Enlightenment is found in the mud—the kind of mud that threatens to suffocate your every breath. Mud that holds you firmly, whose grip paralyzes you. It keeps you hostage to your past limitations while challenging you to be more in the present. It lurks in the dark room in the recesses of your mind where the only possibility for an authentic life exists at the risk of an unknown future, one shrouded in uncertainty and danger as much as potential.

If you engage in the task of personal evolution, you will be challenged. You must come to see yourself as more than you ever thought you could be. It's your only salvation: to be more than you ever thought you could be so you can rise above the grasping fingers of the human condition and joyfully walk into your elemental waters. This cleansing of the soul is enlightenment.

During a chance encounter, I met my navigator for an eight-year journey. On a whim, I made a decision that changed the course of my life. Or perhaps it put me on a path that had already been inscribed in the stars for me to follow.

In April 2012, I met Bolivar Napoleon Luna, Napo as he is known, the brother of the Ecuadorian shaman I had worked with in the States.

Something clicked, like a lightning strike that finds the lone tree on the horizon and ignites it with its fire. It was ancient and familiar, like listening to a song whose words you know even though you can't remember why you know them. I stepped into a chapter of my life that I never expected but had indeed dreamed about. Napo was the navigator who could read the charts, understand the currents, and steer me toward the answers I sought. I was the first mate, ready at the helm, taking instructions and eventually learning to trust my internal compass, the one I had hidden away for so long.

Several deaths and rebirths later, I walk alone on a beach in a small fishing village in Portugal, taking lessons from the ocean and reflecting on what I've learned by walking a path that, for most people, would be seen as courageous. For me, it is simply the path in front of me. I place one foot in front of the other without knowing where it will lead, directed by a truth I have yet to recognize as my own but trusting that my longing will lead me home.

Suffering can be the catalyst to awakening. As I engage the outer world with my work, I become more conscious of the changes within me that have made me more capable, wise, loving, resilient, and courageous than I ever thought I could be. I see versions of my path in those who come to me to do their work. I become the lantern in their darkness, showing them the way and helping them as they stumble.

When I first met Napo, I felt an instant connection, indescribable, quiet, and strong. I didn't need an explanation for it. There was no analysis, nothing at all but a direct connection to this intense feeling.

In his poetry, Rumi writes of his connection to the Beloved. When I met Napo, I realized that for the first time in my life, I had a direct experience of the Beloved. In shamanism, this is called *amor propio*.

Shamanism, the primary wisdom tradition, argues that the universe is controlled through our heartbeats because the Creator placed *amor propio* in our hearts.

I now understand that I was not in love with Napo, yet I was IN(side) LOVE, sourced from the love in me. Napo was the mirror that reflected the light of love I held within myself. His presence was the means through which I expressed that original love. Because he was a shaman and recognized himself as a spiritual and universal being, he could show me the limitless possibility of love within me— and within all of us.

My most significant discovery was that I didn't have to be in a relationship to be in love. I was literally IN love, and love was IN me. It was not out there—outside of me—where someone else could hold love captive.

Relationships fail because we assign love to another person. When we do that, we are hostages to the relationship, forgetting that love is within each of us and belongs to each individual. We forget that our partner is the mirror through which that love is expressed.

Relationships fail when we cannot see the possibility of our own love in the other, or when the other is incapable of—or not ready to see—their inherent potential for love and, therefore, cannot reflect it to us.

Love starts with the self—truly self-love. When we see ourselves as holding the DNA of the divine, of the Beloved, we can no longer deny self-love. That universal, spiritual love is within each of us. We only have to connect to that love within ourselves to be a genuine reflection so others can experience the Beloved. Our most challenging lesson is to learn to love from *amor propio*, which is timeless, limitless, and spiritual in its essence. It begins within.

Allowing myself to feel love again has been difficult. I saw myself fighting it all the way. I didn't want to give in or give over to another until I understood there was no giving in or giving over to another. Instead, it's giving over to myself. It is a gift I can give myself without analyzing the "return on investment" for the love quotient. There is no expectation of return because I'm not falling in love with someone else. Rather, I am falling in love with the being that disappeared— the spiritual being I have been searching for, that I believed I had left behind at birth.

In a moment of vulnerability and openness, I once told Napo I had been searching for him all my life. But I was wrong. I had been searching for the unity of spirit and matter that had dissolved at incarnation.

I knew who I was—the human being made of blood, flesh, and mind—but I had lost the spiritual being that had come to this lifetime, to this earth, to manifest its divinity, creativity, and vital force. I had lost my source.

And now, finally, reflected in everyone around me, I begin to perceive and embrace it, to stop the fighting between the earthbound person and the universal being. I surrender to my essence and discover the path back to the true nature of love.

Love is the true origin of everything. It is the impulse of life to generate more life. Love is the Creator's message and is deeply rooted in respect for all creation. We find the essence of love *through* our relationship with the person we love, who guides us on our path back to our origin.

> *Frente de un amor verdadero, no hay mente ni realidad, solo llanto por la belleza y compasión por el sufrimiento humano.*
>
> —Napo
>
> In the presence of true love, there is neither mind nor reality, only the weeping for beauty and compassion for human suffering.

Human love, like all other human things, is inconsistent. *Amor propio* is constant and never changes. It is not subject to external forces and influences because it is the source of all beginnings and creations, the source of one (singularity) and oneness (totality).

Napo was an enigma, unknown even to himself. Who was he?

Who am I? Who are you? We answer based on the material world, our ego. If we could see ourselves as infinite energy, there would be no answer because there are no limits to spirit. That is our true identity, which most of us have yet to recognize and embrace. We are limitless.

– 26 –
BEGINNINGS

You think you know what tomorrow will bring. You believe that you have the answers to where you're going. The illusion that your life is within your control shatters in an instant, and like a tidal wave, a new life overtakes you. You quickly learn to swim.

It's June 2020, and I'm getting restless. Despite working and hosting retreats for the past year, I feel adrift. Every interaction with Napo causes me distress. My social life is limited to Anna and the volunteers who stay at the property. I don't interact much with the expat community here, and even less so with Ecuadorians. And now there is COVID, which has hit Ecuador very hard. Death is everywhere, and our ability to move around the country is limited to grocery shopping once a week. The world is in chaos. Then my friend Mary Anne calls to check up on me.

"I need to leave Ecuador," I confess. "Things here are bad, but more importantly, there is nothing here for me except reminders of struggle and the situation with Quinta Oasis. I miss so many things. I want a new life!"

"What do you miss?" she asks.

"I miss meaningful conversations. I miss beautiful food—I am done with plantains, fish, and rice! I miss art, culture, and music. And most of all, I miss friends. I have no friends here. If it weren't for my work, I'd go crazy."

"You'd really like Portugal," she states nonchalantly.

"Portugal? Why Portugal?"

"Because it has everything you just mentioned." She adds, "We were there last December. It was warm, fifty degrees, and I know how you hate the cold. The people were so kind. Everything was lit up and joyful, music was everywhere in the streets, and the food and wine—well, the cuisine is amazing!" She describes Portugal so enthusiastically.

"Portugal?" I repeat. "I've been to many European countries but never thought of Portugal."

Within an hour of our phone call, I'm researching life in Portugal. The more I read, the more compelling the idea of moving to Portugal becomes. But my idea of visiting is crushed when I learn that only resident visa holders can enter the country. The country isn't issuing tourist visas due to COVID. "I suppose that means I'll need to get a resident visa," I mumble.

I begin the application process in July. I'm determined to bring my dog, Sophie, so I also start the extensive paperwork required to transport her as an emotional support animal. I submit the paperwork in early October.

In November 2020, the Portuguese government approves my resident visa. I schedule my flight for a few weeks later. Sophie and I will begin a new year and a new chapter by stepping into the unknown with unwavering faith that everything will work out as it should.

I walk the beach in Ecuador the day before my departure, slowly savoring every drop of ocean spray, feeling the gritty sand between my toes and reveling in the warm sunlight as it shines on my face. The tide rises, inviting me to step in. I enter the water as it laps at my ankles, and I give thanks for the time I've spent in the country. Never again will I enter these waters. With each wave comes a new moment to live.

I will soon travel empty-handed, crossing a threshold into a new life with a renewed sense of purpose born of the wisdom and strength that has transformed me. The tide erases my footprints, but the memories linger. I will move from the Pacific Ocean to the Atlantic Ocean. I love the questions that arise from my walks by the sea, regardless of which side of the earth I find myself on. Listening to the waves slamming into the shore, I realize I'm not simply saying goodbye to Ecuador. I'm saying goodbye to me.

After losing myself on another continent, I travel 5,272 miles to Portugal. Only a few years earlier, Ecuador had seduced me with the promise of deep spirituality and a soulful life of purpose. During that time, I watched myself disappear as I merged with a new culture. I didn't notice that as I was melting into my new life, I was also morphing into a stronger woman. Ecuador was a refining fire transmuting the passive woman I used to be, the lost one seeking her place of belonging, into a woman who unapologetically relished inhabiting her own skin.

On December 8, 2020, I fly to Portugal to start anew in a country I have never visited and never planned to visit. My friends have called me courageous to embark on a new solo life in a country where I don't speak the language—especially in the middle of a pandemic. "There's a fine line between courage and crazy," I tell them, "and I'm not sure which side I'm on."

Despite being tired from the long journey, I'm awake as the plane descends. My body wants to move, aching from sitting for hours in recycled air. As the airplane breaks free from the clouds, we circle Lisbon in preparation for landing. The city waves to me from below, entrancing me with her rustic orange rooftops, her labyrinth of winding streets, and *miradouros*—scenic overlooks—perched on her many hills.

I notice her dual personality from my viewpoint in the sky. In the city's center, I glimpse the ageless neighborhoods of Alfama, Baixa, and Chiado, names that meant nothing to me only a few months ago. As we approach the airport, framed by the Tagus River and the Vasco da Gama Bridge, the modern Parque das Nações appears. It was the site of the 1998 World Fair and is now a trendy neighborhood of contemporary buildings and waterfront restaurants. My heart opens to Lisbon's intriguing dual personality, both a revered matriarch of tradition and culture and a youthful woman full of promise and vitality.

Sophie, my dog and companion, lies quietly at my feet, wedged between seats, wrapped in my favorite Ecuadorian sweater. The vibration frightens her when the wheels drop, and I lean down to hold and comfort her. What must she be feeling? Soon she will face new smells, foods, and people. After roaming free on the beach, she must adapt to a more restrictive city environment. I feel a tinge of worry. I'm not sure if I'm worried about having her in a city or if I'm worried about my own adjustment to city life. These thoughts are interrupted by an abrupt thud as the plane lands and taxis. Sophie pulls herself onto my lap and we both peer out the window, which is a portal to our new life. My lungs open to take a deep breath, and only then do I notice I have been holding my breath for a long time.

I arrive at six in the morning, dragging my broken heart, my dog, and my three suitcases. The trip has taken almost twenty-four hours. There's a gnawing in my stomach, and my brain is fuzzy. My first thought is, *I really need coffee.* Sophie and I are both tired, hungry, and badly in need of a bathroom. My fatigue seems out of place with the airport's activity. Everywhere around us, people are arriving and departing. The uniformed staff members are like sheepdogs herding the chaotic masses into the correct queues, pointing out offices, and giving directions in English, Portuguese, Spanish, and languages I cannot identify.

COVID's effects are visible everywhere. Conspicuous bottles of silvery gel sit on every counter. Masked and sometimes gloved staff members route passengers through serpentine lines to check their PCR test results. No one enters Portugal without the required health documentation, as essential as a passport.

Nearby, a family struggles with two small children who are restless and crying. The parents do their best to comfort them, but an overwhelmed parent surely loses a fight with a hungry and tired two-year-old. Speaking quickly in Portuguese, a uniformed woman approaches them. She lifts the cord encircling our queue to bring the family to the front of the line, where they are quickly and sympathetically registered and approved to enter the country.

This is my first glimpse into the nature of the Portuguese people. *How kind and thoughtful*, I think as I watch the family being escorted to the front. Everyone accepts this benevolence as normal. No one seems concerned about line jumping or preferential treatment. Anyone who has had children knows the critical gazes and embarrassment a screaming child creates, yet here it is met with compassion and empathy. "I think I'm going to like it here," I whisper.

Sophie and I finally pass through customs and are met by our driver. Nuno, dressed neatly in a white polo shirt and khaki pants, is a man of about forty, slim, with a happy disposition. "Hello! *Bem vindo a Portugal!*" he calls enthusiastically. In my bedraggled state, I'm unsure if I'm pleased or annoyed by his cheerfulness. Before taking the suitcases, Nuno bends down to cuddle Sophie, who does not protest. I need a shower, a meal, and a nap. I smile involuntarily at Nuno's jovial demeanor and his nonstop talking about how we will love Portugal.

As we drive through the winding streets on the way to an Airbnb in the Arroios neighborhood, Nuno delivers a mini history lesson in near-perfect English. While he tells me about Portugal, and Lisbon specifically, I watch cars weave in and out of excruciatingly narrow streets. I can't help but wonder how the Portuguese navigate these byways without damaging their vehicles.

Nuno continues talking. It's like having a radio on in the background; I'm not paying attention, but I'm aware of him talking. My focus is outside, peering out the van window at the buildings whose architecture echoes Lisbon's history. Despite a devastating earthquake in 1755, Lisbon retains architecture from every period. I see graceful Gothic arches, rich Baroque ornamentation, neoclassical theaters, and Moorish-inspired colors and patterns as we drive through the city.

I'm startled out of my reverie when Nuno hesitantly asks, "Will you remember all this history I tell you?" I assure him I'm impressed with his telling but my head is fuzzy from fatigue. Noticing my avoidance, Nuno offers, "Later, when you settle in, I can take you on tours throughout the city and show you the monuments and plazas, and then you will see how history has formed our great city of Lisbon."

"That would be wonderful, Nuno," I reply with a weak smile. "For now, I think Sophie and I need some rest."

At our destination, Nuno unloads my bags. My Airbnb host meets us, looking like she just got out of bed. She gives us a quick tour of the apartment and quickly identifies local points of interest on a wrinkled, coffee-stained map on the dining room table. Despite my fatigue, I sense a hint of annoyance in her tone. She speeds through the introduction and barely responds to my questions about grocery stores and a local vet. She leaves after a rushed thirty minutes, inviting me to call should I need anything. Feeling more like an intruder than a guest, I make a mental note not to bother her again.

The apartment looks shabbier than it did in the photos online, where the apartment is filled with light and appears clean and modern. The reality is different. The closed shutters keep out the cold but darken the rooms. The furniture is worn and cheap. Even the terrace, the main reason I booked this apartment, is neglected and overgrown with weeds.

But I'm too tired to care. I'm asleep within an hour, dreaming of my new life in Portugal and the adventure I will embark on.

The winter chill keeps me wrapped in a sweater and blanket. Coming from a tropical climate to this damp, chilly apartment feels like an abrupt, if not punishing, change. It has been rainy and cold in the weeks since I arrived. During that time, there has been only an occasional day of sunlight. I thank myself for purchasing a parka before I came. Even Sophie wears a new coat to stay warm, either a soft denim doggie jacket or her red hooded raincoat.

Despite the rain and cold, Lisbon has captured my heart. Like a lover who wraps me in her arms, Lisbon embraces my inner artist by showing off her views of glowing sunsets from the *miradouros* and her geometric patterns in the *calçada* pavement. She invites me to lean in and peer closely at the stories told in the blue *azulejo* tiles. She is vibrant, sensual, and cultured, drawing me into her joie de vivre, teasing me with winding alleys, hidden gardens, and massive fountains.

The sun appears between bouts of rain, and I quickly gather Sophie, my daypack, and my parka to explore the city on foot. Lisbon is truly a walking city if your legs are strong and you don't mind climbing hills to be rewarded with breathtaking views. During the day, we visit parks and plazas, unabashedly claiming the tourist moniker.

About two weeks after arriving in Lisbon, I hire a guide who takes me to explore areas I would never have discovered on my own. Street art covers the walls, and small shops owned by the newest generation of Lisbon citizens tap into the opportunity to make a few dollars with the sparse tourism that has arrived.

I discover a sweet tooth I never knew I had. Sitting at the café near the Castelo de São Jorge with Filipa, my guide, I hear traditional *fado* music from the open window above. The creamy center of the *pastel de nata* melts in my mouth as I savor every bite, slowly teasing the cream from the delicate crust with my tongue. I forget the ache in my legs from climbing the city's many hills. I'm too busy people-watching as I sip my espresso. I listen to the conversations of people passing by my table and hear French, Spanish, Italian, and what sounds like Swedish, all within thirty minutes. "This is why I came here," I remark out loud to no one. With each breath, I fall deeper in love with this city.

Christmas is this week, and I miss my family and friends in the United States. Even though I'm excited about being in Portugal, I can't help but feel lonely. If I were with them, we'd go to see the lights on the Chesapeake Bay and the parade of boats in Annapolis Harbor. A wave of nostalgia washes over me, and I wonder again if I made the right choice by living in Portugal instead of returning to Annapolis, my home in the States.

With each decision, there are remnants of doubt woven into my path. These remnants return to haunt me when memories of what has been—and perhaps could be again—surface to challenge my new life in Portugal. All I can do is choose. Then I take one step at a time toward my uncertain future, trusting that the road is right for me at this moment and acknowledging that there will be other crossroads in my journey where I will make new choices.

Lisbon glows at night with festive holiday lights. The streets are alive with the pulse of hundreds of people. Tonight, people enjoy the Christmas decorations, pausing in the cafés for conversation, coffee, wine, and pastry. Couples stroll arm in arm, leaning their masked faces toward one another. Parents push strollers and delight in the ornaments with their giggling children. The store doors are open to the night air, inviting shoppers to spend their euros on everything from clothes and cookware to toys and art. The COVID Grinch has made only a slight intrusion on the holiday season here. Aside from masked faces, it seems to be a holiday season like all others.

I marvel at the younger crowd navigating the *calçada* streets in their cool black boots and hipster clothes, feeling a twinge of jealousy at their youthful energy. The twenty-foot-tall tree in the Plaza de Rossio, with its red and blue spherical ornaments, draws amateur Instagrammers more concerned with pursing their lips than paying attention to the slight drizzle that has begun. A glowing dome-shaped structure in the Plaza Encarnacão is paired with the word "Lisbon" in mini blue and yellow lights. Lisboetas and tourists alike pose next to the brightly lit decorations for selfies and photos, which they soon post on social media.

Despite the freezing temperatures and the threat of COVID, Lisbon vibrates with life. That vibration captures and enlivens me. I remember the creative person I was in the past—the person I've come here to reclaim. Memories of my years in Ecuador return unbidden as I walk the festive streets. Sorting through them—like sorting photographs—reminds me of why I left. After moving to Ecuador, I didn't feel the vitality there that I feel here tonight. My creativity was stifled by the struggle to build a life of purpose and healing. Fighting the elements, suspicious neighbors, and even my partner tainted my dream of a healing center where the ocean met the mountains. How could I have known that dream was built on an illusion? I never had a chance.

Tonight, loud music and laughter stream through the tiled streets, awakening me to joy and possibility. An older man dances with his wife. Their arms intertwined, they make grand movements. Everyone applauds, and a few couples join them. I sit at a café drinking a small glass of port wine, swaying to the music, and smiling. Such is life in Lisbon. Scenes from a thousand life stories play out on the streets to music and dancing.

− 27 −
THE ALGARVE

I'm not sure which I dislike more: the icy rain that makes sidewalks ridiculously slippery or the constant clouds that dim the light Lisbon is famous for. It's a freezing January day. I'm standing in the kitchen making coffee, wrapped in a blanket, when I decide to break up with Lisbon and move on. The cold shoulder she gives me is too much for my soul, which calls out for the coast's warmth and the ocean's vast expanse.

A friend has tempted me with an invitation to the Algarve, Portugal's southern coast. The Algarve is known as much for its stunning cliffs and wild coastline as it is for drunken tourists and international retirees. I've been hesitating, but Lisbon has left me no choice but to run into the arms of the Algarve with its promise of sunshine and ocean breezes.

"There's a little fishing village in the Algarve where you can spend your days writing and drinking wine," Sage says enthusiastically during one of our phone calls. Sage moved there from the north only a few months previously. "It's quiet, and the landlady is willing to rent you the apartment she used to have as an Airbnb. Because of COVID, no one has rented it, and she prefers a long-term renter instead of the occasional tourist," Sage explains. "I've even negotiated a great monthly rent for you. You must come! It's available starting February 1. What do you say, Alicia?" I can see her smiling on our FaceTime call. We both know I'll say yes. Should there be any doubt, Sage adds, "And Sophie will be able to run free on the beaches too!"

February finds me en route to Ferragudo with Sophie, my luggage, and a hired driver. The irony of going from one fishing village in Ecuador to another in Portugal is not lost on me. I had imagined life in Lisbon, full of art galleries, museum exhibits, dinners with friends, and trips to the Douro vineyards. But despite the enchantment of Lisbon's art and culture, I find myself longing to connect to the natural world where the ocean tides remind me that all things have their ebb and flow and the birds sing day and night, in joy and sorrow. This paradox between continuance and impermanence has marked my life for the past eight years. Perhaps I've changed more than I thought? Now the idea of mornings watching the fishermen return with their catch and quiet evenings watching the sun set over the horizon draws me inward and back to my self, like returning to a place I had forgotten, even if I'd never been there before.

Ecuador had been like that at the beginning. Its natural beauty entranced me. I loved sitting on the balcony in the mornings, the sun casting its rays from behind the house to shine onto the gardens, the birds singing their morning songs, and me in my hammock chair drinking my coffee with my four dogs lying at my feet. Those memories are sweet but distant, as if I had dreamed them. But like all dreams, they dissolve into the stark light of reality, echoing my wishes and rippling out through time.

After a three-hour ride where David, my driver, shares his vast knowledge of Portugal, I arrive in Ferragudo. Virgo, my landlady, is waiting with a friendly smile as we park on the street outside the building. "Welcome to Ferragudo!" she exclaims. Her pronounced Irish accent explains the twinkling eyes. If it weren't for the masks we wear and the omnipresent threat of disease, I'm sure we would have hugged for a long time.

David brings the luggage to the second-floor apartment I will call home. After a few words of greeting with Virgo, he departs for his three-hour drive back to Lisbon. Sophie has bounded up the stairs and is already sniffing the apartment.

"Well, I know you'll be enjoying our lovely village of Ferragudo!" Virgo exclaims. With Irish hospitality seeping from her words, she says, "It's been quiet now with COVID, but the people are lovely. Tommy and I are only a few streets away, and we'd be happy to help you settle in should you need anything." She gives me a tour of the apartment and carefully points to the wine chilling in the refrigerator, the *pastel de nata* (cream pastry) on the counter, and the bag of coffee sitting beside the espresso machine. I am drawn to the fresh flowers on the living room table, a thoughtful touch of welcome. All the windows are open to the fresh air. Colorful art brings joy into the space, and the large balcony door invites me out to look at the street below and the ocean in the distance. The brightness of the apartment stands in stark contrast to the cold, gloomy Airbnb in Lisbon. I breathe a sigh of relief. This was the right decision.

"I know you're sensitive to the cold, so I've put an electric blanket on the bed," Virgo says. "You simply turn it on a few minutes before you're ready to sleep, and you'll slip into a nice, toasty bed." I want to kiss her at that moment, anticipating how different this will be from getting into a cold, damp bed in Lisbon, where the portable radiator was a poor substitute for heat.

She points to a large bowl on the dining table. It's filled with the most enormous oranges I've ever seen. "These are local oranges from Silves. They make great juice. And here is the juice maker," she says, opening one of the kitchen cabinets. "Fresh juice for your breakfast!"

Virgo spends about an hour showing me all the cabinets in the well-stocked kitchen and teaching me how to turn on the bathroom floor heat and open the windows. A natural conversationalist, she has what the Irish call the "gift of gab."

"Well, I'll leave you now. I'm sure you're tired from your ride. I'll check in with you tomorrow." She says her goodbye with the same enthusiasm as her welcome. The door barely closes before I fall asleep on the bed next to Sophie.

I know what it's like to wake up in a place I've never been yet immediately recognize it as home. Coming to Ferragudo is like that. Still hovering near sleep, I slip out of the warm blankets of my new bed, anticipating rich, dark Portuguese coffee streaming from the espresso machine sitting prominently on the counter. There is still a chill in the air, but I have heat today and throughout the winter months. The season passes, gradually melting into the warmth of June.

Like a flower blossoming, my life unfolds in this small fishing village in the Algarve. Sophie and I greet every morning in the field bordering the Rio Arade as it changes from an estuary to a river flowing from Silves and past Portimão toward the Atlantic Ocean. I pause on the opposite shore to watch Ferragudo come alive. The fishermen reweave their nets. Tourists walk the dock area to take photographs, and beachgoers, with their umbrellas and towels, make their way through town for a day at Praia Grande.

A thousand conversations happen at any moment if you are open to hearing them. Birds singing, seagulls squawking, and the whisper of the reeds in the breeze all speak to me. I see a gray mare, owned by the area gypsies, grazing just below the path I'm walking with Sophie. My tongue *click-clicks* an invitation. I'm surprised when the mare lifts her head and responds with a whinny. Slowly, the massive animal approaches, her round belly grazing the tall grasses as she steps over the uneven ground and climbs to meet me on the dirt path.

She hovers over me. Her gentle eyes peer into mine, belying the heft of her body. They speak of her pain at the hard work she is forced to do and the joy she finds in her foal, which is now half her size.

She nuzzles my shoulder like my mother, Mina, did when she wanted to wake me in the mornings. The horse's eyes remind me of how my mother would look at me just before she shared a tidbit of wisdom. I want to lose myself in those eyes as I did when I was a child listening to my mother sing, pray, or laugh.

My hand caresses her neck as I lean into her shoulder in an embrace she welcomes. We speak in the unspoken language that arises when two hearts connect. It's a timeless place where both humanity and animals once understood this type of connection. Now, it seems that only a few of us can hear the symphony of wordless conversations surrounding us. "Thank you for blessing me with your presence," I whisper to the mare. She leans into me in response.

We stand together in this timeless bubble on the banks of a river I am coming to know well. The world is going about its business, but she and I are simply present to one another.

Sophie barks her impatience, perhaps jealous of this new friend I've made. "I must be going now," I tell the mare. When I turn around, she is still following me—and does so until she reaches the spot where the path becomes a road to the parking lot. I walk toward her and embrace her with a promise to return. She turns and walks toward her foal, who is grazing nearby. Sophie and I continue our walk home, passing the cafés now crowded with locals and tourists enjoying their coffee and break-fast. We cross the small bridge over the canal and head to the apartment, as we do every day in this new place I call "home for now."

I arrive at my apartment and settle in for a day of work. My laptop whirs to life. As it logs on, it flashes a reminder for the day: *Mina died today, June 26, 2017.* I had not realized the date. The mare's eyes appear before me and morph into my mother's. I'm engulfed by memories of the woman whose wisdom taught me to see beyond the obvious and not to fear the unknown. I explode into tears, releasing the grief that has been hiding for a long time.

Sitting on this dock in Ferragudo reminds me of a port in Ecuador that I frequented several years ago to distract myself from a dream that was dying. Today, with my coffee in hand, I watch the seagulls dive-bomb the Algarvian fishermen, waiting for a sliver of fish or an unwanted crustacean to be thrown into the sea. I'm smiling this time, watching the fishermen yell at the birds and joke with each other. Ferragudo has been a surprise in the same way that the pimpled boy next door grows into a handsome man. A bit unexpected and rough around the edges but authentic and down-to-earth.

There is little pretense in the people here. The aproned woman who sells me bread corrects my Portuguese, smiles, then places an extra cookie in my bag. The older fisherman who grills tonight's *peixe* on the dock outside the fanciest restaurant calls to me as I walk by with Sophie. He says, "*Tudo bem?*" Smiling, we bump fists as I walk past. "*Sim, tudo bem,*" I respond. The bar owner sets down a glass of red wine before I even order it as I watch the sun surrender to the evening over a glistening ocean. They know me here in a way that never happened in Ecuador.

The memory of my last walk arises, reminding me of the ocean's lesson, showing me with the ebb and flow of the tide that each wave changes me. Each moment is here, then gone. Each footprint will eventually disappear, even as I keep walking into my life.

For now, Portugal is my home—a place where I'm seen for the person I am becoming. With winks and smiles, the people here have taught me that home is what I carry with me as I leave behind what binds me. I have paused here in this little village in the Algarve, knowing that, if only for now, this is where I belong.

Tudo bem!

– 28 –
DEATH BY TEXT

I recognize the phone number on my screen, blinking, insisting I answer.

"Hello?" I answer tentatively.

"Hello, Alicia. It's Megan." Her voice comes through my computer speakers. I haven't spoken to her in years. While I was in Ecuador, I only called her once—to ask for help. She refused and blamed me for the trouble I had caused between the brothers. We used to be close, but now, every hair on the back of my neck stiffens at her voice.

Avoiding any pleasantries, I respond, "Yes, I know. I recognized your number. What happened? Why are you calling me?"

"Napo is dying," she states. "He's in a coma in a hospital in Quito. Carlos is with him."

I stop breathing. My head bows, and my body collapses into the mesh office chair that normally sustains me in a healthy posture. Slowly but firmly, I feel the surge of grief rise from my gut into my solar plexus, travel up to my heart, then move into my throat.

"What happened?" I ask in a broken voice as I fight back tears.

"A few weeks ago, he was diagnosed with prostate cancer. Then, about five days ago, his legs swelled. Carlos took him to the hospital. They were doing surgery when he had a brain embolism. There's nothing they can do for him. He's in palliative care. There's no brain activity, and his organs are slowly shutting down."

Napo and I had so many conversations about life and death. Sitting on the balcony at our property, looking out to the ocean as the sun set, enjoying a splash of whiskey to end our day, he'd muse, "Death is a doorway to the cosmos, to the place of *gozo*, back to my origin, back to my true home. When the time comes, I will welcome the journey. As far back as I can remember, I have longed to return." There it was, that longing in his eyes that I would see when he didn't think I was looking. It appeared during those times when he might hold one of the dogs, absently petting it, or when he would stand on the beach with his arms outstretched, reaching for the sky as his feet dug into the sand and sea.

"That was his worst nightmare," I say to Megan. "He would never want this. He is in the in-between space. It is awful for him." I imagine his soul suffering, begging to fly to the infinite, where he will again meet his Creator and return to his essence. What could he be waiting for?

I cry at the thought of his imprisonment. All the grief I believed I had worked through flares again. My chest tightens. I struggle to open my throat, fearing the grief might choke me. I thought this was over. I believed I had processed all of this. Yet here it is again, reminding me of my loss, my suffering, and my deep wounds, which are invisible but nevertheless ever-present.

The memory of our bonding at Cochasquí surfaces, like a short video. It happened many years ago, when we first began our relationship. "We will forever be connected," he had said. "Through time and space, this bond between you and the shaman transcends all."

This deep connection has always existed and will continue in some liminal space where mortal hands can never touch it. At the time, I did not realize the significance of the ritual at the top of the pyramid. It wasn't until years later, when we were at our best, that I could feel him no matter where we were. On those early mornings, at around four o'clock, I would wake up in bed in the United States and feel his presence in the room. Sometimes I even felt the mattress shift, as if someone had been sitting at the foot of the bed.

I'd sensed something a week before Megan's phone call. I had been recovering from COVID, and the medicine caused erratic sleep and disturbing dreams. Early one morning, I woke with a premonition of his death. I attributed it to my anxiety and the disruptive sleep I was experiencing as I healed from the virus.

Megan speaks again, but the words float, dissipating like bubbles that children blow and pop. "Alicia? Alicia, are you there?"

"Yes, sorry. Yes, I'm here." Slowly, my mind begins to function again. I recover quickly, moving to solutions and setting aside any emotions that might interfere.

"I won't go to Ecuador," I say clearly. "Carlos is with him, I assume. Obviously, you know I live in Portugal since you called me," I add. "I'm easy to find on the Internet."

"Yes, that's how I found your phone number." She hesitates for a moment, and I sense there is something else she wants to ask.

"What is it?" I prompt her.

"Carlos wants to know what you plan to do with the property," she says tentatively.

"I'm sure he does," I reply with a hint of cynicism that I can't hide. I'm not surprised they are concerned about our property. However, according to Ecuadorian law, the property belongs solely to me.

When I left in 2019, I wondered if I would ever recoup my investment. After presenting Napo with several potential buyers and seeing his resistance to showing the property, I gave up on the idea that I would ever see a dime from selling. And now, his impending death presents the possibility of recovering the funds I invested in building Quinta Oasis.

I recall the day we finished the pool. We went for our first swim in it together, playing like two children in the water, stark naked in the twilight and having fun diving and pushing one another. We wrapped ourselves in our robes and sat in the outdoor kitchen on the terrace above the pool to enjoy a cold beer and the warm breeze.

"We built this," Napo said. "One day, we will not be here. I want us to make a promise to one another."

"Sure, what is it?" I asked, not recognizing the importance of the promise we would make—the evening's joy was so far removed from the issue of mortality.

"I want you to promise me that if I die before you and you sell the property, which I assume you would, you will contribute to my brother Carlos. He has influenced our relationship, cared for me all his life, and contributed toward this property. And in return, if you die, I promise to contribute to your son Joseph. Can we make that promise now to each other?"

Still reveling in the joy of our swim together, I playfully put out my hand, extending my pinky. "Pinky swear. Yes. I promise."

He looked at me in confusion.

"It's something we Americans do sometimes when we make promises. Give me your pinky finger." He looked at me with a touch of skepticism that changed to a smile when I wrapped our pinky fingers together. "Now say, 'I pinky swear that we will take care of Carlos and Joseph if something happens to us.'"

"Okay, Alicia. Pinky swear, *sí te prometo y me prometes*." And so, the arrangement about the property was made, an understanding that I knew I would honor.

"What are you thinking of doing about the property?" Megan asks again.

"Many years ago, I promised Napo that if he died before me, I would take care of Carlos. I intend on keeping that promise."

I hear her sigh of relief. "That will bring much peace to Carlos during this difficult time. He told me he did not have the energy to fight with you."

I smile; her indication that he was ready to fight me for the property does not surprise me. "I gave up on that bullshit a long time ago, Megan. I never expected to see a dime after I left. I have a beautiful life now, and I refuse to ruin it by expending time, money, or energy on the past. So tell him I will sell it and work with my attorney in Ecuador to do this. But now is not the time for this conversation. I'm sure Carlos is devastated at his brother's impending death, his mentor, and the only person he ever really loved. I know that Napo loved and trusted only Carlos during his life. I'm sure it is the same for Carlos."

"Yes, I agree," she affirms. "I know that their relationship was unique. It was always the two of them against the world. They only slightly trusted me, and I always knew that Napo was first for Carlos in everything."

"Put his mind at ease that I will honor my agreement with Napo about the property." It is time to finish this call.

My brain reacts to set my boundaries and to relate my promise carefully. Now, alone in my office, I slump into the chair. Gradually, the grief returns. I go into the kitchen for a glass of water, then sit in the living room and look out the balcony windows toward Monchique, the mountain framed by the sliding doors. Tears become sobs that wrack my body as I rock to comfort myself where no comfort can be found. I sob for about thirty minutes, until I feel depleted. Then my brain shuts off for the rest of the day. I decide not to avoid the emotions but to stay with whatever arises.

The next day at 1:30 p.m., I receive a text from Megan. It reads: *Napo died last night. I know you need a copy of the death certificate to move forward on the sale of the property.*

That is all it says. It feels like a sneaky gut punch, like when you know you'll be hit but you don't expect it to come in that manner. I don't answer it until ten o'clock that night: *Btw. Your text was probably the most callous, inhumane text I have ever received.*

The next day, I walk hand in hand with my sadness on the nearby cliffs. Returning to my balcony, I pour a glass of wine and watch the sunset. I offer a toast to the shaman who had been a part of my life and played a role in making me who I am today. "I loved you, Napo. You will always have a space in my heart. *Vaya con Dios, mi amor,*" I call as I lift my glass in the fading light.

− 29 −
EL AMOR VENCE TODO

If green were a smell, it would smell of dank leaves and sweet bark. It would feel like moist air and sound like buzzing insects.

It's just as I remember it. The rainforest changes, yet it doesn't change. It dies and is reborn in its own image. Perhaps once reborn, it is more than it was before—more verdant, more humid. Where it is untouched by man, you still sense the vital life force emanating from the ground, rising into your body like a tingling electric current, recharging and teasing you with a taste of what it means to be alive.

I follow the path through the brush—the one I remember from years ago. I don't slip and fall like before. Wet branches slap my face as if to say, "Wake up, you've been sleeping again." The mud grabs at my rubber boots, sucking them down even as I lift my feet to take another step. I keep walking, looking for the opening where the branches pull away, allowing me to approach the river below.

After a few minutes, I hear the gurgling sound of water flowing over large boulders that the earth placed there eons ago. The sound becomes louder as I continue. Insects relentlessly buzz in my ears even though I swipe at them. They win. I stop flailing my arms and gaze toward the sound of the river as it becomes louder, now more of a gushing than a gurgling.

Through the branches, I glimpse the river. Years ago, it had been depleted, appearing more like a creek than a river that had once been home to fish, frogs, and other jungle life. Today it is full, coming up to the bank. The sun's rays find their way through the dense brush, illuminating the surface, making it sparkle by playing on the vegetation that dances in the flow.

That's when I see Napo standing on the other bank, in the shadow of the trees, waiting for me. I climb down from one last ledge in the riverbank and sit on the large rock, the same one I sat on when I visited this sacred place with his brothers many years ago.

"It's you. I wondered if you would be here," I call across the water.

"I came to say goodbye. Panterita, I am not man any longer. I am spirit." He affectionately uses the name he gave me when we met.

I shift my position on the boulder so I can see him clearly. He isn't more than twenty feet away, on the river's opposite bank. He looks different. I once saw a photograph of him when he was young. He looks like he did in that photo. His tanned face has yet to wrinkle. His nose has not yet been broken in a fight. His curly black hair, which I had loved to twirl in my fingers when we made love, is longer, just below the shoulder. He wears a colorful bandana around his forehead. There's no sweat coming from his face, a sharp contrast to my own state; my shirt is painted with oval-shaped wet spots, and sweat glues my hair to my neck. His white cotton shirt, embroidered with two strips of rainbow colors, hangs over his jeans. He looks fit and strong, and much younger than he did when I last saw him. He stands in the moss barefoot.

"Napo, what is it like to die? Did it hurt?" I ask.

He breathes deeply but doesn't move. His hands are pushed into his jeans pockets. "To die is to be free again, Panterita. The body that kept me imprisoned needed to go through its demise, to break down molecule by molecule so I could be fully released. That took a few days, but I was already outside it."

"Napo, I miss the man you were before the darkness. I loved you so deeply that I lost myself in you," I confess to both of us.

"It is possible that we lost ourselves in each other," he replies. "Do you still recall my teachings? Can you remember the lessons on *totalidad* and *unidad*? Have you understood the power of *amor propio*? Are you still conscious of the feminine and masculine energy within you? Do you still speak to the Creator on full moon nights?"

He does not chide me. Instead, he reminds me in the way he used to when we were so united, deeply in love with the human and spirit we both were. He used to say there were three of us: Him, Me, and Us. Those moments when we were "Us" were profound, steeped in shamanism, allowing us access to metaphysical dimensions we had not reached individually but could reach when we were strong together.

"It has taken a long time for me to heal, Napo. First, I had to forgive you. Then, more importantly, I had to forgive myself to find my way back to my soul." I am calm as I say this. I am not angry or sad.

He senses this and replies, "We were destined to meet, Alicia. We were destined to learn from each other and from our suffering. I shared with you what I never shared with anyone. My gift to you was the wisdom of the soul, shamanic teachings passed down for generations. We were the encounter between two bright stars clashing, merging, and ultimately destroying one another to birth a new life. This is where the universal movement brought us, to this spot at my river, where you first learned that your life was not your own. The beginning of a journey for you and now the end of our journey together on this planet."

"Will I ever see you again?" I ask.

"We are never alone when there is consciousness, when we face genuine encounters of the soul. Even if we are apart, the universe will always keep us connected." It is as if the sound of the river diminishes; the flow calms so I can hear his voice coming to me on the breeze in that lilting cadence that had always entranced me.

"Napo, do you remember at Cochasquí, at the pyramid where we were bonded, what you whispered in my ear?" I don't wait for him to respond. "You said, '*El amor vence todo.*' Those exact words were inscribed on a small piece of paper in the locket I wore that day. 'May love prevail.' Perhaps that is what brings us here now. Outside time or space, we always knew this truth."

"There is wisdom in your words, Panterita. Keep growing, and never forget who you are and where you come from. Do not forget your cosmic beginnings, your spiritual memory. I will always love you, not as a human, but from the divine origin from where we all come. I will see you one day on my side of the river. When ready, the tunnel of time will open for you to pass through. I will be waiting for you on the other side." He raises his arm and opens his palm to me. I stand and reach toward him, my palm out as if to meet his. For a moment, I feel the thickness of his hand against mine. He closes his hand, lowers his arm, turns, and slowly disappears into the rainforest.

Sophie's wet nose presses against my cheek. She paws at me, insisting I wake up, shoving herself under my sheets to push me out. I lean over to grab my phone. It reads 8:30 a.m. My face is moist with tears. Where have I been?

The memory of the rainforest comes back clearly, as if I have just returned from a trip. I appease Sophie by cuddling with her, leaning against my pillows to remember every detail of my last encounter with Napo. I spend about fifteen minutes reviewing my dream, allowing myself to feel the emotions that were absent while I was in the trance state. Once I am calm and renewed, I go to my laptop and write down every detail.

This evening, Sophie and I walk on the cliffs in Ferragudo to watch the sunset. It is a warm August evening, and the sun drops toward the horizon at about 8:30 p.m. I watch as the orange orb descends until it disappears into the ocean. A slight breeze makes me wrap my arms around myself. I stand on the cliff's edge, grateful for my life as the sky lights up in gold, orange, and purple hues. I sense Napo standing next to me, just behind my left shoulder, watching the sunset as we had done on the coast of Ecuador. His presence is palpable. As the light slowly dims, I feel Napo's life force follow the sunset into the ocean, his spirit returning to the sea of universal consciousness that he had longed to reunite with.

"*El amor vence todo,*" I call out loud. The wind carries my words beyond the horizon, back to the one who whispered them to me on an ancient pyramid in Ecuador.

Acknowledgments

Every story has its beginnings, and this one started with a blank page and a writer's determination. Yet, a story is never truly solitary; it's a tapestry woven with characters, places, and emotions. To bring *The Shaman's Wife* to life took more than my solitary efforts; it took a community.

I'm grateful for the invaluable support from individuals who believed in this story. Your encouragement, insights, and unwavering faith in me lifted me up during moments of self-doubt. Your contributions to this journey have been immeasurable.

First and foremost, I would like to express my profound gratitude to Amy Gigi Alexander, my writing coach and mentor. Her guidance, from the vibrant surroundings of San Miguel de Allende, reshaped the narrative and pushed me to fully embrace the story. She not only taught me the craft of writing but also granted me the freedom to explore new and unconventional ways of expression.

My deep appreciation goes to Brooke Warner and Linda Joy Myers, whose memoir writing program equipped me with the skills and confidence to proudly call myself a writer.

To my dear friend, Michelle Thomas, the owner of Quinta Carvalhas in Santarém, Portugal, thank you for providing a sanctuary where I could delve into the most challenging chapters of this memoir.

Your tranquil quinta, with its horses, meditation gardens, and natural beauty, offered solace during the darkest writing moments.

I am grateful for the wordsmiths whose editing transcended the words on the page to capture the essence of the mystical experiences woven into this narrative.

A heartfelt thanks to my friend, Leslie Craig, whose meticulous attention to detail was invaluable in preparing the final manuscript.

To everyone else who offered comments, encouragement, and feedback along the way, even if your names aren't mentioned here, your contributions were sincerely appreciated.

Lastly, I bow in gratitude to the women in my life. Your encouragement and feedback reassured me that this book has the potential to resonate with women who, like me, have faced the challenge of reclaiming their power and agency. Your support fuels my passion to continue writing stories that can make a positive difference.

About the Author

photo credit: Mary Gardella Photography

Alicia M. Rodriguez is a seasoned executive coach and the author of two inspiring books, *Everyday Epiphanies: Insights for Living with Purpose* and *Manage Your Life Before Life Manages You: More Joy and Less Stress in 365 Days.* Her writing has also been featured in numerous online publications, including Thrive Global, Wilde Magazine, Tiny Buddha, Substack, and Medium. She believes that we are spiritual beings having a human experience, a perspective that has led her from corporate boardrooms to the rainforests, mountains, and coast of Ecuador, where she spent six years with an Ecuadorian shaman. Alicia currently resides in Ferragudo in the stunning Algarve region of Portugal, where her morning cliff walks with her dog, Sophie, inspire her creativity and bring her joy and peace.

You can learn more about Alicia on her website at
www.aliciamrodriguez.com

Looking for your next great read?

We can help!

Visit www.shewritespress.com/next-read
or scan the QR code below for a list
of our recommended titles.

She Writes Press is an award-winning
independent publishing company founded to
serve women writers everywhere.